The Art of War: What Sun Tzu Actually Teaches About Strategy

How to Think Clearly About Conflict, Competition, and Advantage

Ancient Wisdom Hacks

Published by NX, Inc.

Copyright © 2026

Table of Contents

PART II

THE DECISION PRIMITIVES

(The irreducible components of all strategic decisions)

PART III

THE ORDER OF DECISION

(Why sequence matters more than intelligence)

PART IV

FAILURE MODES

(How the system breaks when misused)

PART V

APPLICATION WITHOUT TACTICS

(How this framework is used without collapsing into advice)

Chapter 23: Why _The Iliad_ Is Required
Humans break systems
Pride destroys alignment
Cost is paid by people, not models

Closing

THE ROLE OF THE ART OF WAR FRAMEWORK

Final positioning
 What the framework is
 What it is not
 Why precision—not boldness—is the outcome

Preface

Purpose of the Framework

This book exists for one reason: to formalize **The Art of War** as a *decision system*.

Not a philosophy.
Not a historical artifact.
Not a collection of motivational aphorisms repackaged for modern taste.

A system.

The premise is simple and severe: when decisions carry real cost, when information is incomplete, when time is constrained, and when errors compound rather than reset, intuition and inspiration fail. Character fails. Optimism fails. Even intelligence fails. What remains is structure—or the absence of it.

This framework answers a single governing question:

How are decisions made correctly when error is irreversible, pressure is constant, and the margin for recovery is narrow or nonexistent?

That question is not theoretical. It is not philosophical. It is operational. It arises in business acquisitions, capital allocation, leadership under uncertainty, conflict resolution, negotiation, litigation strategy, organizational restructuring, and personal decisions where reputation, leverage, or survival are at stake.

Most modern interpretations of *The Art of War* avoid this question. They soften the text. They aestheticize it. They turn it into metaphor. In doing so, they miss what the original work actually is: a procedural manual for minimizing loss in adversarial environments.

Ancient Wisdom Hacks (AWH) exists to correct that error.

The Misunderstanding of *The Art of War*

For centuries, *The Art of War* has been misunderstood because it is concise, unsentimental, and resistant to embellishment. Its language is compact because it assumes competence. Its tone is cold because the subject demands it. And its logic is ruthless because the consequences of failure are final.

Sun Tzu does not write to inspire courage. He writes to prevent catastrophe.

The opening line of the text is not aspirational. It is diagnostic:

> "War is a matter of vital importance to the State; the province of life or death; the road to survival or ruin."

This is not rhetoric. It is scope definition.

From the first sentence, the author establishes that decisions made under these conditions cannot rely on hope, emotion, or moral posturing. They require structure—because the cost of being wrong is existential.

Modern readers often recoil from this framing. They want lessons about leadership style, mindset, or confidence. They want stories about bold action and decisive strikes. They want victory narratives.

The Art of War is uninterested in all of that.

It is interested in *avoidance*.
In *delay*.
In *containment*.
In *error reduction*.

The most quoted lines of the text are also the most misunderstood:

> "The supreme art of war is to subdue the enemy without fighting."

This is not pacifism. It is cost accounting.

Fighting is expensive. Fighting introduces variance. Fighting multiplies unknowns. Therefore, fighting is a failure condition—not a goal.

Yet most modern interpretations begin where Sun Tzu ends: at action. This framework reverses that error.

AWH Positioning: Framework Over Philosophy

Ancient Wisdom Hacks treats classical texts not as sources of inspiration but as *compressed systems*—dense operational logic designed for environments where failure could not be explained away.

AWH language is precise by necessity. Vagueness is a liability. Ambiguity is a hidden cost.

This framework assumes the reader does not need to be motivated. It assumes the reader already understands that outcomes matter. What the reader needs is a way to *think correctly under pressure*—before action is taken and before damage is done.

The purpose of this framework is not to make you feel capable. It is to make your decisions *less fragile*.

That distinction matters.

What This Framework Is

This book formalizes *The Art of War* as a **decision system composed of interlocking primitives**, governed by order of operations, constrained by failure conditions, and optimized for cost containment rather than triumph.

It treats decisions as processes, not moments.

1. It Defines Decision Primitives

A decision primitive is an irreducible unit of judgment—an element that must be evaluated regardless of context, scale, or domain.

In *The Art of War*, these primitives are not hidden. They are stated explicitly:

> "The art of war is governed by five constant factors..."

These factors—often translated as Moral Law, Heaven, Earth, the Commander, and Method and Discipline—are not virtues or ideals. They are variables. Each represents a domain of risk that must be assessed *before* engagement.

This framework strips away poetic translation and treats these factors as operational categories:

- Alignment and cohesion
- Timing and external conditions
- Terrain and structural constraints
- Leadership reliability
- Systems, logistics, and execution capacity

A decision that ignores even one of these primitives is incomplete. An incomplete decision is not neutral—it is dangerous.

This framework maps these primitives to modern environments: markets, organizations, negotiations, legal contexts, and personal strategic decisions.

2. It Establishes an Order of Operations

One of the most critical—and most ignored—elements of *The Art of War* is sequencing.

Sun Tzu is explicit:

> "He who knows when he can fight and when he cannot, will be victorious."

This is not about bravery. It is about *timing within a process*.

Most failures occur not because the wrong action was taken, but because the right action was taken *out of sequence*. This framework enforces order:

1. Assessment before commitment
2. Position before engagement
3. Information before movement
4. Cost before ambition
5. Action as a consequence, not an impulse

In modern contexts, this means due diligence before acquisition, leverage before negotiation, structure before scaling, and exit planning before entry.

The framework rejects urgency as a virtue. Speed without structure is not decisiveness—it is exposure.

3. It Identifies Failure Conditions

Most strategic systems focus on success criteria. *The Art of War* focuses on **defeat conditions**.

Sun Tzu repeatedly warns against identifiable patterns of failure:

> "There are five dangerous faults which may affect a general..."

These are not character flaws. They are predictable cognitive errors: recklessness, cowardice, temper, sensitivity to honor, and overprotectiveness.

Translated into modern terms, they become:

- Overconfidence
- Risk aversion at the wrong stage
- Emotional reactivity
- Ego-driven decision-making
- Attachment to sunk costs

This framework treats failure conditions as constraints. If a decision triggers one of these conditions, it is flagged regardless of potential upside.

The goal is not to win brilliantly. The goal is to avoid losing catastrophically.

4. It Prioritizes Cost Containment Over Victory

Victory is a misleading metric. It is often visible only in hindsight and frequently masks long-term damage.

Sun Tzu is clear:

> "There is no instance of a nation benefiting from prolonged warfare."

Victory that consumes resources, morale, time, or optionality is not victory—it is delayed failure.

This framework measures decisions by:

- Irreversibility
- Resource depletion
- Optionality loss
- Exposure to second-order effects

A decision that "wins" but destroys future flexibility is treated as a failure within this system.

5. It Treats Action as a Late-Stage Consequence

Action is the *final* stage of decision-making, not the beginning.

Sun Tzu emphasizes preparation repeatedly:

> "Victorious warriors win first and then go to war, while defeated warriors go to war first and then seek to win."

This is not metaphorical. It is procedural.

Winning occurs at the level of structure, information, and positioning—long before action is visible. By the time action occurs, the outcome should already be constrained.

This framework formalizes that logic. If action feels dramatic, it is already too late.

What This Framework Is Not

Clarity requires negation. This book does not attempt to be everything, and it explicitly rejects several common expectations.

It Does Not Inspire

Inspiration is volatile. It decays under pressure. It creates confidence without structure.

This framework assumes that if you are reading it, you already understand the stakes of your decisions. You do not need emotional reinforcement. You need a system that holds when emotion fails.

It Does Not Motivate

Motivation is irrelevant when cost is real.

Sun Tzu never asks whether soldiers feel motivated. He asks whether supply lines hold, whether intelligence is accurate, and whether timing is correct.

This framework operates on the same assumption: discipline outperforms desire.

It Does Not Provide Tactics

Tactics are context-dependent and perishable. A tactic that works in one environment may fail catastrophically in another.

The Art of War deliberately avoids detailed tactics because they invite imitation without understanding.

This framework follows that discipline. It provides decision structure, not recipes.

It Does Not Promise Success

Any system that promises success under uncertainty is fraudulent.

Sun Tzu offers no guarantees. He offers *probability management*.

This framework does the same. It reduces exposure. It narrows loss. It improves decision quality. Outcomes remain contingent.

It Is Designed to Reduce Irreversible Error

This is the core objective.

Success is not guaranteed. Survival is not guaranteed. Advantage is not guaranteed.

What *can* be managed is the frequency and severity of irreversible mistakes.

This framework exists to minimize those.

Why This Matters Now

Modern environments reward speed, visibility, and confidence. They punish hesitation and ambiguity. This creates a systemic bias toward premature action.

Social media celebrates bold moves. Business culture glorifies decisive leaders. Narratives focus on winners and erase the cost of their failures.

The Art of War is incompatible with this culture.

It assumes that most losses are self-inflicted. That exposure is optional. That conflict is often entered unnecessarily. And that restraint is a form of intelligence.

AWH reintroduces this discipline into modern decision-making.

How to Use This Framework

This book is not meant to be read once. It is meant to be *applied repeatedly*.

It is a reference system. A checklist. A constraint map.

You will return to it when decisions feel urgent. When information is incomplete. When pressure is applied to act quickly.

When that happens, this framework does not ask, *What do you want to do?*

It asks:

- What is known?
- What is unknown?
- What is irreversible?
- What is being risked unnecessarily?
- What failure condition is being ignored?

Only after those questions are answered does action become permissible.

Closing Orientation

Sun Tzu ends his treatise with a warning about intelligence, secrecy, and foreknowledge. He does not conclude with triumph. He concludes with discipline.

This framework follows that precedent.

It is not dramatic.
It is not comforting.
It is not flattering.

It is functional.

And when cost is real, function is the only metric that matters.

PART I

THE CONDITIONS OF STRATEGIC REALITY

(Why decisions fail before they begin)

Chapter 1

Constraint Is the Default State

Introduction: The Error That Precedes All Others

Most decisions fail before they begin.

Not because the actor is foolish.
Not because the plan is weak.
Not because the environment is hostile.

They fail because the decision-maker begins from a false assumption: that *freedom* is the default condition, and constraint is an obstacle to be overcome.

This assumption is so deeply embedded in modern thinking that it often goes unnoticed. Business literature frames opportunity as abundance. Leadership culture frames choice as empowerment. Strategy is marketed as expansion, leverage, and upside.

But **The Art of War** begins from the opposite premise.

Sun Tzu does not assume abundance.
He assumes scarcity.
He does not assume freedom of action.
He assumes restriction.

And because of that, his system survives reality.

This chapter establishes the foundational condition of all strategic thinking: **constraint is not a problem to be solved; it is the environment in which all decisions already exist**.

If this premise is misunderstood, every decision that follows—no matter how clever—will be structurally flawed.

Constraint Is Not a Temporary Condition

Modern decision-making frameworks often treat constraint as a phase:

- "Once we raise capital…"
- "Once we have better data…"
- "Once we get buy-in…"
- "Once the market opens up…"

Constraint is framed as a temporary limitation on an otherwise open field.

This framing is incorrect.

Constraint is permanent.

The form may change—time today, information tomorrow, tolerance the day after—but **there is no decision state in which all variables are favorable**. To wait for such a state is not patience; it is avoidance disguised as prudence.

Sun Tzu assumes this from the outset. His text never imagines a battlefield with unlimited resources, perfect intelligence, or infinite time. Every principle he introduces presumes restriction.

> "The general who advances without coveting fame
> and retreats without fearing disgrace… is the jewel of
> the kingdom."

This is not a moral statement. It is a recognition of constraint: reputation, fear, and ego all reduce freedom of action. The commander who acknowledges these pressures—and is not ruled by them—retains *relative* flexibility, not absolute freedom.

AWH language is precise here: **relative flexibility is the maximum achievable state**. Absolute freedom does not exist in strategic reality.

No Decision Occurs in Abundance

Abundance is a narrative convenience, not an operational condition.

In real decision environments:

- Time is limited or asymmetrical.
- Information is partial, delayed, distorted, or intentionally misleading.
- Resources are finite and often already committed.
- Attention is fragmented.
- Tolerance—organizational, psychological, political—is narrow and volatile.

These are not edge cases. They are the baseline.

Sun Tzu states this indirectly but repeatedly. Consider:

> "If you know the enemy and know yourself, you need not fear the result of a hundred battles."

This line is often misread as a promise of certainty. It is not. It is an admission of scarcity.

To "know" in Sun Tzu's language does not mean omniscience. It means *knowing enough*. It means operating under incomplete information but compensating through structure, discipline, and restraint.

The fact that Sun Tzu specifies *both* the enemy and the self reveals the constraint: knowing one without the other is insufficient, and knowing both fully is impossible. Strategy therefore operates in a narrow corridor between ignorance and overconfidence.

Abundance thinking collapses under this reality.

Scarcity of Time Is the First Constraint

Time is not merely limited; it is **unevenly distributed**.

Some actors face immediate deadlines. Others benefit from delay. Some decisions decay rapidly. Others improve with patience. The critical error is assuming time is neutral.

Sun Tzu is explicit:

> "There are roads which must not be followed, armies which must not be attacked, towns which must not be besieged..."

Why? Because time interacts with terrain, morale, supply, and weather. A decision that is *possible* is not necessarily *permissible* within the time available.

AWH reframes time not as a countdown clock but as a **compression force**. As time compresses, optionality collapses. The later a decision is made, the fewer viable paths remain—regardless of intelligence or intent.

Most modern failures stem from misreading this dynamic:

- Waiting too long to exit a bad position.

- Acting too quickly without allowing constraints to surface.
- Confusing urgency with importance.

Time scarcity is not solved by speed. It is managed by sequencing.

Scarcity of Information Is Structural, Not Accidental

Information asymmetry is not a flaw in the system. It *is* the system.

Sun Tzu treats intelligence as precious, costly, and inherently incomplete:

> "What enables the wise sovereign and the good general to strike and conquer… is foreknowledge."

Foreknowledge does not mean certainty. It means **advantageous partial knowledge**.

Information arrives late. It arrives filtered. It arrives corrupted by bias, fear, incentives, and deception. Strategic actors do not wait for perfect information; they design decisions that remain viable *despite* its absence.

This is why *The Art of War* emphasizes deception:

> "All warfare is based on deception."

This is not cynicism. It is realism. If deception is possible, information must be treated as provisional. If information is provisional, decisions must be reversible where possible and constrained where not.

AWH principle: **the less reliable the information, the more conservative the commitment must be**.

Abundance thinking ignores this. It assumes more data will arrive in time. Strategy assumes it may not.

Scarcity of Tolerance: The Hidden Constraint

One of the least discussed constraints is tolerance—organizational, political, psychological, or cultural.

Every system has a breaking point:

- Stakeholders lose patience.
- Teams fracture.
- Markets punish hesitation.
- Opponents exploit hesitation.
- Internal resolve degrades.

Sun Tzu addresses this obliquely when discussing morale, discipline, and command unity. Armies collapse not only from defeat, but from exhaustion, confusion, and loss of confidence.

> "If troops are punished before they have grown attached to you, they will not prove submissive; and, unless submissive, they will be practically useless."

Tolerance is finite. It must be conserved like any other resource.

A decision that is technically correct but exceeds tolerance limits will fail operationally. AWH treats tolerance as a *hard constraint*, not a soft consideration.

Freedom of Action Is Always Limited

Freedom of action is not a starting condition; it is an outcome—and a fragile one.

Every choice forecloses others. Every commitment narrows the field. Every visible move invites reaction.

Sun Tzu warns repeatedly against overextension:

> "He will win who knows when to fight and when not to fight."

This is not restraint for its own sake. It is preservation of freedom. By not acting prematurely, the commander maintains optionality.

AWH reframes freedom of action as **decision slack**—the ability to absorb error without collapse. Slack is created through restraint, not aggression.

Most failures come from spending slack too early.

Opportunity Is a Secondary Condition

Modern strategy worships opportunity. *The Art of War* treats it as incidental.

Opportunity is not sought; it is recognized. And it is recognized only because constraints have been mapped correctly.

Sun Tzu states:

> "Opportunities multiply as they are seized."

This line is often misused to justify aggressive action. In context, it means something else entirely: **opportunity emerges from correct positioning within constraint**, not from reckless expansion.

You cannot exploit opportunity you cannot sustain. You cannot sustain what exceeds your constraints.

Therefore, AWH inverts the usual framing:

> **Opportunity does not define strategy. Constraint does.**

Why Decisions Fail Before They Begin

Decisions fail at inception when:

1. Constraint is denied or minimized.
2. Scarcity is reframed as temporary rather than structural.
3. Freedom of action is assumed rather than protected.
4. Opportunity is prioritized over survivability.
5. Action is treated as progress rather than exposure.

These failures are not tactical errors. They are *premise errors*.

Sun Tzu's system avoids them by beginning from constraint. Every calculation, every movement, every deception is built on the assumption that resources are limited, time is hostile, and error compounds.

The Core Principle Restated

All strategy begins inside constraint, not opportunity.

This is not pessimism. It is realism.

Constraint defines the battlefield.
Constraint defines the decision space.
Constraint defines what is possible, permissible, and survivable.

A decision that ignores constraint is not bold. It is blind.

A decision that acknowledges constraint gains clarity, discipline, and endurance.

This chapter establishes the ground on which all subsequent analysis rests. Until constraint is accepted as the default state, no framework—ancient or modern—can function as intended.

In the chapters that follow, we will formalize how constraint shapes evaluation, sequencing, and action. But none of that is possible until this foundational error is corrected.

Strategy does not begin with what you *want* to do.

It begins with what you *cannot afford* to do.

And everything else follows from there.

Chapter 2

Cost Exists Before Action

Introduction: The Illusion of the First Move

Most decision-makers believe cost begins at the moment of action.

They are wrong.

Action does not *create* cost.
Action merely **reveals** the cost that was already embedded in the situation.

This misunderstanding is one of the most consistent sources of strategic failure across domains: business, warfare, negotiation, leadership, and personal decision-making under pressure. When cost is treated as a consequence rather than a condition, decisions are framed too narrowly, evaluated too late, and justified too optimistically.

The Art of War does not make this mistake.

Sun Tzu treats cost as antecedent, not emergent. He assumes that every possible action already carries a burden—material, temporal, psychological, political, or structural—*before* it is taken. The purpose of strategy is not to avoid cost, but to **see it clearly**

**enough to choose which costs are survivable and which are
not**.

This chapter formalizes that principle.

Cost Is a Precondition, Not a Penalty

Modern frameworks often imply that cost is incurred *after* a
decision is executed: expenses are logged, losses are measured,
and consequences are reviewed post hoc. This framing subtly
absolves the decision-maker of responsibility for costs that
"unexpectedly" arise.

Sun Tzu allows no such absolution.

He opens his analysis of warfare by emphasizing logistics, supply,
and economic strain—long before describing movement or
engagement:

> "The rule is, not to besiege walled cities if it can
> possibly be avoided… the preparation of mantlets,
> movable shelters, and various implements of war, will
> take up three whole months."

This passage is rarely quoted in modern summaries, precisely
because it is unglamorous. Yet it reveals a critical truth: **the cost
of a siege exists before the siege begins**. Time, materials,
morale, and political capital are already committed the moment the
option is considered.

Action does not generate these costs. It only exposes them to consequence.

AWH language is explicit: **if a cost surprises you, it was not unforeseen—it was unexamined**.

The Myth of the Clean Start

Decision-makers often speak as though each choice begins from a neutral baseline:

- "If this doesn't work, we'll pivot."
- "We can always walk away."
- "The downside is limited."

These statements are rarely true.

There is no clean start. Every decision is layered atop prior commitments, sunk costs, reputational stakes, institutional inertia, and cognitive bias. These factors are already active before action occurs.

Sun Tzu acknowledges this layering implicitly when he warns against prolonged conflict:

> "There is no instance of a nation benefiting from prolonged warfare."

Prolongation is not caused by a single bad move. It is caused by cumulative cost that was tolerated, rationalized, or ignored early on. Each extension of commitment makes exit more expensive than entry, until action becomes compulsory rather than chosen.

The initial error is not overextension. It is **underestimating pre-existing cost**.

Hidden Cost as the Primary Failure Vector

Visible costs are rarely fatal. Hidden costs are.

Visible costs include:

- Direct financial expenditure
- Overt resource allocation
- Measurable time investment

These are the costs decision-makers account for because they are legible and reportable.

Hidden costs include:

- Loss of optionality
- Reputational exposure
- Internal morale erosion
- Attention fragmentation
- Strategic signaling to competitors or adversaries
- Normalization of escalation

Sun Tzu repeatedly warns against these indirect consequences, though his language is austere:

> "He who is prudent and lies in wait for an enemy who is not, will be victorious."

"Lying in wait" is not passivity. It is **cost containment**. By delaying action, the commander avoids revealing intent, exhausting troops, or committing resources prematurely.

Hidden cost is dangerous precisely because it is difficult to quantify. Yet it is almost always the deciding factor in failure.

AWH principle: **what you cannot measure will cost you the most**.

Most Losses Occur Before Contact

One of the most counterintuitive insights of *The Art of War* is that defeat often occurs without a battle.

Sun Tzu states plainly:

> "The skillful leader subdues the enemy's troops without any fighting."

This is not simply about psychological warfare or diplomacy. It reflects a deeper structural truth: by the time forces meet, the outcome has largely been determined by prior positioning, logistics, intelligence, and morale.

In modern terms, most losses occur:

- During flawed due diligence
- Through mispriced risk
- By overcommitting too early
- By signaling weakness or desperation
- By exhausting tolerance before leverage is secured

Contact—whether a negotiation, acquisition, lawsuit, or market entry—merely *confirms* what has already been decided by these earlier conditions.

Action is not the battlefield. Preparation is.

Cost Revealed, Not Created

To say that cost is revealed by action is to shift responsibility backward, where it belongs.

Consider Sun Tzu's treatment of terrain:

> "He who occupies the field of battle first and awaits his enemy is at ease; he who comes later to the scene and rushes into the fight is weary."

The fatigue of the late-arriving force is not caused by the fight itself. It is caused by the *conditions under which the fight is entered*. The cost—fatigue, disorder, vulnerability—exists prior to contact and is merely exposed when action begins.

AWH reframes this dynamic universally: **action is a diagnostic tool**. It exposes the reality of costs that were already present but insufficiently examined.

This is why premature action is so dangerous. It forces revelation before containment.

Cost and Irreversibility

Not all costs are equal. The most dangerous costs are those that cannot be undone.

Sun Tzu's emphasis on avoiding unnecessary engagement reflects an acute awareness of irreversibility:

> "If you lay siege to a town, you will exhaust your strength."

Exhaustion is not easily reversed. Neither is reputational damage, loss of trust, nor depletion of capital reserves. Once incurred, these costs constrain all future decisions.

AWH categorizes costs along a critical axis:

- **Reversible vs. irreversible**
- **Delayed vs. immediate**
- **Visible vs. hidden**

Strategic failure often occurs when reversible costs are overestimated and irreversible costs are discounted. The framework insists on the opposite bias: *assume irreversibility until proven otherwise.*

Cost and Information Asymmetry

Cost is also asymmetrically distributed. Some actors bear it immediately; others defer it. Some can absorb it; others cannot.

Sun Tzu implicitly accounts for this when he discusses intelligence and deception:

> "When able to attack, we must seem unable; when using our forces, we must seem inactive."

Why? Because revealing capability too early imposes cost without extracting value. It invites countermeasures and erodes surprise.

Information asymmetry magnifies cost. The less you know, the more expensive mistakes become. The more you reveal, the more others can shift cost onto you.

AWH principle: **never pay full price for incomplete information.**

The Accounting Error in Modern Strategy

Modern organizations are structurally biased to underestimate cost because accounting systems privilege what is quantifiable.

Balance sheets do not capture:

- Strategic distraction
- Leadership bandwidth
- Cultural decay
- Loss of credibility

Sun Tzu's system predates modern accounting, yet it accounts for these factors implicitly by focusing on endurance, morale, and discipline.

> "In war, then, let your great object be victory, not lengthy campaigns."

Victory here is not conquest. It is *closure*. Ending exposure is often more valuable than extending advantage.

AWH reframes this as **cost horizon management**: how long can this decision impose burden before it becomes self-defeating?

Why Decision-Makers Act Despite Unclear Cost

If unclear cost is so dangerous, why do decision-makers act anyway?

Because action provides emotional relief. It feels decisive. It creates momentum. It resolves ambiguity—even if the resolution is destructive.

Sun Tzu is acutely aware of this temptation. His text repeatedly warns against impulsive engagement driven by anger, pride, or impatience:

> "The general who is choleric and quick-tempered may be provoked by insults."

Emotional drivers collapse cost analysis. They substitute short-term psychological comfort for long-term survivability.

AWH language is blunt: **urgency is not a justification; it is a warning signal**.

Framework Rule Formalized

If cost is unclear, action is premature.

This is not a suggestion. It is a rule.

Clarity does not mean certainty. It means that:

- The categories of cost are identified
- Irreversibility is acknowledged
- Hidden costs are surfaced
- Tolerance limits are estimated
- Exit conditions are defined

Only then does action become permissible.

Sun Tzu never advocates paralysis. He advocates *deliberate engagement*. When cost is understood, action can be swift and decisive precisely because uncertainty has been reduced to survivable bounds.

The Strategic Discipline of Non-Action

One of the most radical implications of this chapter is that **non-action can be the most cost-effective decision**.

Sun Tzu legitimizes restraint:

> "To fight and conquer in all your battles is not supreme excellence; supreme excellence consists in breaking the enemy's resistance without fighting."

Breaking resistance often means waiting while costs accumulate *for the other side*. Time, morale, resources—these are not neutral. They decay differently depending on position.

Non-action, when chosen deliberately, is not passivity. It is **cost displacement**.

Cost as the True Terrain

This chapter reframes cost as the true terrain on which strategy operates.

Geography matters. Markets matter. Opponents matter. But beneath all of these lies cost: who bears it, when, how much, and whether it can be reversed.

Sun Tzu understood this intuitively. AWH makes it explicit.

Before any decision, the strategist must ask:

- What costs already exist?
- Which will be revealed by action?
- Which cannot be undone?
- Who is bearing them now?
- Who will bear them after contact?

Until these questions are answered, movement is not courage—it is exposure.

Closing Orientation

Most strategic disasters are later explained as execution failures. This is comforting and false.

They are cost-analysis failures.

They occur because decision-makers treat cost as an afterthought rather than a prerequisite. They move before the terrain of cost is mapped. They confuse action with progress.

The Art of War does not make this error. Neither does this framework.

Action is not the beginning of strategy.
Cost analysis is.

And when cost is unclear, the correct move is not to advance—but to wait.

Chapter 3

Information Is Always Incomplete

Introduction: The Fantasy of Knowing Enough

Every strategic failure begins with a quiet, usually unspoken assumption:

If we just had better information, this decision would be easy.

This assumption is false.

It is not false because decision-makers are careless or under-resourced. It is false because **perfect intelligence does not exist**, and more importantly, **it never has**. Strategy does not operate in the absence of information, but it also never operates with completeness.

The Art of War is explicit on this point. Sun Tzu does not write for a world in which truth is fully observable and reliably transmitted. He writes for a world in which information is delayed, distorted, strategically manipulated, and cognitively misread.

This chapter formalizes a foundational condition of strategic reality:

> **Information is always incomplete, and it is incomplete by structure, not by mistake.**

Any framework that treats uncertainty as a temporary inconvenience rather than a permanent condition will fail under pressure.

Perfect Intelligence Does Not Exist

The desire for perfect intelligence is understandable. It promises safety. It promises justification. It promises control.

But it is a mirage.

Sun Tzu never promises certainty. Instead, he repeatedly emphasizes *relative advantage* in knowledge:

> "What enables the wise sovereign and the good general to strike and conquer… is foreknowledge."

This line is often misunderstood. "Foreknowledge" is not omniscience. It is *asymmetric awareness*. It is knowing *more* than the adversary, or knowing *sooner*, or knowing *what matters* when others do not.

Perfect intelligence would eliminate strategy entirely. If outcomes were certain, decision-making would be mechanical. Strategy exists precisely because knowledge is partial.

AWH language is direct: **uncertainty is not a flaw in strategy; it is the reason strategy exists at all**.

The Structural Nature of Incompleteness

Information gaps persist not because intelligence systems fail, but because reality itself generates delay, distortion, and loss.

Sun Tzu understands this implicitly when he writes about spies, deception, and secrecy. An entire chapter of *The Art of War* is devoted to intelligence—not because intelligence can be perfected, but because it is costly, fragile, and contested.

> "Spies are a most important element in war, because on them depends an army's ability to move."

If intelligence were complete and reliable, spies would be unnecessary. The very existence of espionage is proof of structural incompleteness.

Information is incomplete because:

- Events unfold faster than they can be observed
- Actors conceal intent
- Signals are filtered through intermediaries
- Incentives distort reporting
- Cognitive bias reshapes perception

None of these conditions can be eliminated. At best, they can be managed.

Delay Is Not an Error—It Is a Condition

One of the most dangerous misconceptions in modern decision-making is the belief that information delay is a temporary failure of systems or processes.

It is not.

Delay is structural.

Sun Tzu repeatedly references timing, distance, terrain, and communication as limiting factors. Messages take time. Troops take time to move. Intelligence takes time to gather and verify.

> "He will win who knows how to handle both superior and inferior forces."

Handling forces requires knowing their condition—but that knowledge is always *out of date* by the time it is acted upon.

In modern contexts, the same dynamic applies:

- Financial reports lag reality
- Market data reflects past behavior
- Organizational sentiment is discovered after it has shifted
- Opponent strategy is inferred after it has evolved

Information is always historical by the time it reaches the decision-maker.

AWH principle: **you are always deciding about the present using the past**.

Noise Is Inseparable from Signal

If information were merely incomplete, the problem would be manageable. The deeper issue is that information is also *contaminated*.

Signal does not arrive cleanly. It arrives embedded in noise.

Sun Tzu addresses this through his emphasis on deception:

> "All warfare is based on deception."

Deception works because observers cannot easily distinguish truth from misdirection. Even honest information is mixed with error, bias, exaggeration, and omission.

Noise enters the system through:

- Conflicting reports
- Overinterpretation of minor data points
- Emotional framing
- Political incentives
- Selective disclosure

Modern decision environments amplify noise through speed and scale. More data does not mean more clarity. Often, it means more distraction.

AWH language is precise here: **clarity is not achieved by accumulation, but by filtration**.

Why More Information Often Makes Decisions Worse

There is a persistent belief that increasing information volume improves decision quality. In practice, it often degrades it.

Sun Tzu never advocates exhaustive data collection. He advocates *relevant* intelligence.

> "If you know the enemy and know yourself, you need not fear the result of a hundred battles."

This is not a call for infinite knowledge. It is a call for *correct framing*. Knowing what matters—and ignoring what does not—is the strategic skill.

More information introduces new risks:

- Analysis paralysis
- False precision
- Overconfidence
- Delayed action beyond optimal windows

AWH principle: **information that does not change your decision criteria is noise, not insight**.

Interpretation as the Core Strategic Skill

If certainty is impossible, then decision quality cannot depend on certainty.

It depends on **interpretation**.

Interpretation is not guesswork. It is structured inference under constraint. It involves:

- Weighting incomplete signals
- Discounting unreliable sources
- Accounting for bias (your own and others')
- Identifying what *must* be true for an action to be viable

Sun Tzu frames this obliquely when discussing command competence:

> "The general who thoroughly understands the advantages that accompany variation of tactics knows how to handle his troops."

Understanding variation means recognizing that conditions are fluid and information is provisional. The commander does not wait for clarity; he *interprets ambiguity correctly*.

AWH reframes interpretation as **probability management**, not prediction.

The Danger of Waiting for Certainty

Waiting for certainty feels responsible. It is often reckless.

By the time certainty arrives, options have narrowed, costs have risen, and adversaries have adapted.

Sun Tzu warns against delayed action, but his warning is conditional:

> "There are five essentials for victory…"

None of them include certainty. They include preparation, discipline, alignment, and timing.

The strategist who waits for complete information surrenders initiative. The one who acts without interpretation surrenders survivability.

The discipline lies in acting when uncertainty has been reduced to *acceptable bounds*, not eliminated.

Information Asymmetry and Power

Information is not merely incomplete; it is unevenly distributed.

Some actors know more. Some know sooner. Some know what matters.

Sun Tzu treats intelligence as a competitive domain:

> "Hence it is that which none in the whole army are
> more intimate relations to be maintained than with
> spies."

Information asymmetry creates leverage. But only if it is
interpreted correctly.

Possessing information without understanding its implications is
not an advantage—it is a liability. Misinterpreted intelligence leads
to false confidence, misaligned action, and catastrophic exposure.

AWH principle: **information advantage without interpretive
discipline accelerates failure**.

The Illusion of Objectivity

Modern decision-makers often assume that data is neutral and
interpretation is optional.

This is incorrect.

All data is framed. All data is contextual. All data is collected for a
reason, by someone, under constraints.

Sun Tzu never separates intelligence from intent. Spies are not
neutral observers; they are instruments of strategy.

> "Be subtle! Be subtle! And use your spies for every
> kind of business."

Subtlety implies interpretation. It implies reading not just what is reported, but *why* it is reported and *what is not being said.*

AWH language emphasizes this: **there is no raw data, only data embedded in motive.**

Cognitive Bias as an Information Filter

One of the most underestimated sources of noise is the decision-maker's own mind.

Sun Tzu identifies this indirectly through his warnings about temperament:

> "If a general shows confidence in his men but always insists on his orders being obeyed, the gain will be mutual."

This reflects an awareness that ego, fear, pride, and impatience distort perception. Decision-makers see what they want to see. They discount what threatens their narrative.

Incomplete information interacts with bias to produce false clarity. This is more dangerous than acknowledged uncertainty.

AWH principle: **confidence in interpretation must always be lower than confidence in structure.**

Why Interpretation Must Be Systematic

Because information is incomplete, delayed, noisy, and biased, interpretation cannot be intuitive alone.

It must be systematic.

This framework enforces interpretive discipline by:

- Separating signal from urgency
- Distinguishing reversible from irreversible decisions
- Stress-testing assumptions
- Asking what information *would* change the decision—and whether it is likely to arrive in time

Sun Tzu's system is procedural, not emotional. He does not trust instinct unmoored from structure.

> "The general who loses a battle makes but few calculations beforehand."

The failure is not lack of intelligence, but lack of *pre-interpretation*—the absence of a framework to make sense of incomplete data.

The Implication Formalized

Decision quality depends on interpretation, not certainty.

Certainty is unattainable. Interpretation is unavoidable.

The strategist who accepts this does not demand perfect information. He demands *sufficient clarity to act without catastrophic exposure.*

The strategist who rejects this waits, hesitates, overanalyzes—or acts impulsively when pressure becomes unbearable.

Strategic Restraint in an Uncertain World

Sun Tzu's preference for restraint is not rooted in caution, but in epistemology. He understands that action amplifies error when interpretation is weak.

> "He who is prudent and lies in wait for an enemy who is not, will be victorious."

Waiting is not about time. It is about *interpretive readiness*. When understanding is sufficient, action becomes efficient and decisive.

AWH reframes restraint as **information discipline**.

Closing Orientation

This chapter dismantles a dangerous myth: that better decisions require better certainty.

They do not.

They require better interpretation.

Information will always be incomplete. Delay will always exist. Noise will always contaminate signal. Bias will always distort perception.

These are not obstacles to strategy. They are its operating environment.

The Art of War does not seek to escape uncertainty. It teaches how to function within it.

This framework does the same.

You will never know enough.
You will never see everything.
You will never act with certainty.

And yet, decisions must still be made.

The quality of those decisions will depend not on what you know—but on how well you interpret what you do not.

Chapter 4

Time Is Not Neutral

Introduction: The Most Mispriced Variable

Time is the most misunderstood variable in strategy.

It is treated as neutral.
It is treated as linear.
It is treated as something that can always be "made up for" with speed, effort, or intensity.

This belief is false—and costly.

Time is not a backdrop against which decisions unfold. It is an **active force** that reshapes cost, information, leverage, morale, and optionality with every passing moment. It rewards some postures and punishes others. It amplifies preparation and exposes haste. It compounds error as efficiently as it compounds advantage.

The Art of War does not treat time as a neutral resource. It treats it as a weapon—sometimes wielded, sometimes endured, always respected.

This chapter formalizes a core condition of strategic reality:

**Time is never neutral. It is either working for you
or against you, depending entirely on posture.**

Any framework that equates speed with decisiveness or delay with
weakness is structurally incapable of surviving real pressure.

Time as a Force Multiplier

In modern discourse, time is often reduced to a metric: deadlines,
timelines, quarters, schedules. Strategy literature frequently urges
leaders to "move fast," "act quickly," or "outpace competitors."

Sun Tzu never issues such blanket advice.

Instead, he differentiates between **movement at the right time**
and movement at the wrong time—between speed that
compresses cost and speed that multiplies it.

> "He will win who knows when to fight and when not to
> fight."

This sentence is not about courage. It is about timing.

To "know when" implies that time alters the equation. The same
action taken today may be disastrous, while the same action taken
tomorrow may be decisive—or unnecessary.

AWH language is precise here: **time changes the cost profile of
every decision**.

Time Increases or Decreases Cost Depending on Posture

Time does not affect all actors equally.

This is the first critical distinction.

For one side, time may reduce cost by allowing:

- Information to surface
- Opponent morale to erode
- Resources to accumulate
- Structural advantages to solidify

For the other side, the same passage of time may increase cost by:

- Bleeding capital
- Losing credibility
- Allowing competitors to reposition
- Creating internal doubt or fatigue

Sun Tzu repeatedly emphasizes posture over motion:

> "He who occupies the field of battle first and awaits his enemy is at ease; he who comes later and rushes into the fight is weary."

The difference is not speed. It is *posture*.

One side uses time to settle, prepare, and conserve. The other spends time reacting, compressing decisions, and absorbing fatigue.

Time magnifies posture. It does not correct it.

The False Equivalence of Speed and Decisiveness

Modern culture glorifies speed. Fast decisions are framed as strong decisions. Delay is framed as weakness or indecision.

This is a profound strategic error.

Speed is a mechanical property.
Decisiveness is a structural one.

Sun Tzu never equates the two.

> "The general who wins a battle makes many calculations in his temple before the battle is fought."

Calculation takes time. Preparation takes time. Alignment takes time.

What appears decisive in execution is often the result of prolonged restraint beforehand.

AWH language rejects the cult of speed: **fast action taken from poor position is not decisiveness—it is exposure.**

Speed as Cost Acceleration

Speed compresses time. Compression amplifies error.

When decisions are rushed:

- Information is interpreted poorly
- Hidden costs surface too late
- Irreversibility is underestimated
- Emotional drivers override structure

Sun Tzu warns explicitly against impulsive speed driven by emotion:

> "The general who is choleric and quick-tempered may be provoked by insults."

Provocation creates urgency. Urgency invites haste. Haste converts manageable situations into irreversible losses.

Speed is not inherently bad. But it must be earned through preparation. When speed precedes structure, it becomes a cost multiplier.

Delay Is Not a Single Thing

One of the most dangerous simplifications in strategy is treating delay as uniformly negative.

Delay is not one condition. It has two fundamentally different forms:

1. **Delay as leverage**
2. **Delay as decay**

Confusing the two is fatal.

Sun Tzu distinguishes them implicitly throughout his work. He praises waiting when it strengthens position, and condemns waiting when it exhausts resources.

> "There is no instance of a nation benefiting from prolonged warfare."

This is not a condemnation of patience. It is a condemnation of *unproductive delay*—delay that consumes strength without improving position.

AWH language formalizes this distinction.

Delay as Leverage

Delay is leverage when time improves your relative position.

This occurs when:

- Your costs are low and stable
- The opponent's costs are rising
- Information asymmetry favors you
- Optionality is preserved or expanded

In these conditions, waiting is not passive. It is *strategic pressure.*

Sun Tzu legitimizes this posture:

> "He who is prudent and lies in wait for an enemy who
> is not, will be victorious."

"Lying in wait" is not avoidance. It is positioning.

AWH reframes this as **asymmetric patience**—the discipline of allowing time to burden others while you remain structurally intact.

Delay as Decay

Delay becomes decay when time erodes your position faster than it erodes the opponent's.

This occurs when:

- Resources are being consumed without return
- Morale or confidence degrades
- External conditions worsen predictably
- Internal tolerance limits are approached

In these cases, waiting is not strategic restraint. It is **deferred loss**.

Sun Tzu warns against this indirectly through his emphasis on supply lines, morale, and endurance. An army that waits while starving is not exercising discipline—it is collapsing slowly.

AWH language is explicit: **delay without positional improvement is decay, not caution.**

Why Decision-Makers Misread Time

Time is misread for three primary reasons:

1. **Psychological discomfort with uncertainty**
2. **Cultural pressure to appear decisive**
3. **Misalignment between visible and invisible costs**

Speed relieves anxiety. Delay sustains it. Organizations often choose speed not because it is correct, but because it feels resolving.

Sun Tzu understands this temptation and warns against it by emphasizing discipline over emotion.

> "If soldiers are punished before they have grown attached to you, they will not prove submissive."

Rushed decisions fracture trust. Fractured trust accelerates decay. Time magnifies this effect.

Timing Versus Urgency: A Critical Distinction

This chapter introduces a non-negotiable distinction:

Timing ≠ urgency

Urgency is emotional.
Timing is structural.

Urgency arises from pressure, fear, ego, or external expectation. Timing arises from analysis of cost, information, posture, and leverage.

Sun Tzu never urges action because time is running out. He urges action because conditions are favorable.

"Move not unless you see an advantage; use not your troops unless there is something to be gained."

Advantage is a structural condition, not an emotional one.

AWH formalizes this as a rule: **urgency is not evidence; it is noise**.

Time and Information Decay

Information decays over time—but not uniformly.

Some information becomes obsolete quickly. Other information becomes clearer with delay. The strategist must know which is which.

Sun Tzu accounts for this through his emphasis on intelligence and foreknowledge. He understands that acting on stale intelligence is often worse than acting with less information but better timing.

AWH principle: **the value of information is inseparable from timing**.

Acting too early may mean acting blind. Acting too late may mean acting on yesterday's truth.

Time as a Revealer of Structure

Time exposes structural weaknesses.

Organizations that rely on momentum collapse when momentum slows. Strategies that require constant success fail when conditions fluctuate. Leaders who depend on charisma falter under prolonged pressure.

Sun Tzu's preference for discipline over heroics reflects this understanding.

> "In war, discipline is more important than numbers."

Discipline survives time. Inspiration fades.

AWH reframes this insight: **if your strategy cannot tolerate time, it is already broken**.

Time and Optionality

Time interacts directly with optionality.

Every moment that passes without commitment preserves options—*if* costs are contained. Every moment that passes under exposure narrows options.

Sun Tzu repeatedly emphasizes avoiding irreversible commitment:

> "Do not press a desperate foe too hard."

Why? Because desperation collapses options—for both sides.

Timing decisions must therefore account for how time affects exit paths, reversibility, and future leverage.

AWH principle: **good timing preserves options longer than it commits them**.

The Strategic Use of Slowness

Slowness is not the absence of speed. It is the *presence of control*.

Sun Tzu's system is not fast by default. It is measured.

"Victorious warriors win first and then go to war."

Winning first takes time. It requires preparation, deception, alignment, and patience.

Only after these are secured does speed become useful.

AWH language reframes slowness as **pre-decisional discipline**.

When Speed Becomes Necessary

This chapter does not argue against speed categorically.

Speed is essential **after** timing has been achieved.

When posture is strong, costs are mapped, and interpretation is sufficient, speed prevents counteraction. At that point, delay invites risk.

Sun Tzu recognizes this balance:

"Let your rapidity be that of the wind."

But note the sequence: rapidity follows preparation.

Speed without timing is reckless. Speed with timing is decisive.

Why Most Strategic Failures Misdiagnose Time

After failure, decision-makers often say:

- "We waited too long."
- "We moved too fast."
- "The window closed."

These statements are usually incomplete.

The failure was not timing—it was **misreading posture**.

Time did not betray the decision. The decision failed to account for how time would reshape cost, information, and tolerance.

AWH language is blunt: **time does not cause failure; misunderstanding time does**.

Time as a Strategic Weapon

Sun Tzu uses time offensively as well as defensively.

By forcing opponents to wait, overextend, or rush, he shifts cost onto them.

> "If the enemy is taking his ease, give him no rest."

Rest here is not physical comfort. It is *strategic stability*.

Time can be weaponized to destabilize, exhaust, or expose.

But only when posture allows it.

Closing Orientation

This chapter dismantles another dangerous simplification: that time is neutral and speed is strength.

Time is active.
Time is asymmetric.
Time magnifies structure.

Sometimes it rewards patience.
Sometimes it punishes delay.
Sometimes it demands speed—but only after discipline.

The strategist does not ask, *How fast can we move?*

He asks:

- How does time affect cost right now?
- Who benefits from waiting?
- Who bleeds from delay?
- Is urgency structural—or emotional?

Until those questions are answered, movement is not decisiveness.

It is guesswork under pressure.

And *The Art of War* was never written for guesswork.

PART II

THE DECISION PRIMITIVES

(The irreducible components of all strategic decisions)

Chapter 5

Cost

Introduction: Why Cost Comes First

Every strategic framework claims to evaluate cost.

Most of them lie—unintentionally, but consistently.

They treat cost as an accounting line item, a forecast, a downside scenario, or a post-decision reconciliation. In doing so, they miss what **The Art of War** treats as foundational: **cost is not a consequence of strategy; it is the terrain on which strategy operates**.

Sun Tzu does not begin with goals.
He does not begin with vision.
He does not begin with victory.

He begins with *burden*.

"War is a matter of vital importance to the State; the province of life or death; the road to survival or ruin."

This is not rhetoric. It is cost framing.

From the first sentence, Sun Tzu defines the domain as one in which losses are real, irreversible, and often asymmetric. Any system that evaluates decisions without first decomposing cost is not strategic—it is aspirational.

This chapter formalizes **Cost** as the first decision primitive: an irreducible element that must be evaluated *before* action, *before* opportunity, and *before* intent.

Why Cost Is a Primitive

A decision primitive is something that cannot be reduced further without breaking the system.

Cost qualifies because:

- Every action carries cost, regardless of outcome
- Cost exists prior to execution
- Cost compounds even when action is delayed
- Cost constrains future decisions more than failure does

Sun Tzu implicitly treats cost this way throughout his work. He does not ask whether an action *can* be taken. He asks whether it is *worth what it will consume.*

AWH language is unambiguous: **if you do not understand cost at the primitive level, you are not making a decision—you are making a wager.**

The Strategic Definition of Cost

Within this framework, cost is not limited to money, casualties, or resources.

Cost is anything that reduces future freedom of action.

This includes:

- Capital depletion
- Time consumption
- Attention diversion
- Morale erosion
- Reputation exposure
- Political or organizational tolerance loss
- Optionality collapse

Sun Tzu repeatedly emphasizes that the most dangerous costs are not immediate losses, but *long-term constraints*:

> "There is no instance of a nation benefiting from prolonged warfare."

Prolongation is costly not because battles are lost, but because *endurance is consumed*. The longer exposure continues, the fewer choices remain.

This is the strategic meaning of cost.

Direct Cost vs. Indirect Cost

Direct Cost

Direct costs are immediate, visible, and usually quantifiable.

They include:

- Financial expenditure
- Manpower allocation
- Time blocks
- Material usage

Sun Tzu references these explicitly when discussing logistics:

> "The preparation of mantlets, movable shelters, and various implements of war, will take up three whole months."

These costs are obvious—and therefore, often overemphasized.

Indirect Cost

Indirect costs are secondary, delayed, and often unmeasured.

They include:

- Loss of focus on higher-value objectives

- Internal fatigue or disengagement
- Normalization of escalation
- Strategic signaling to adversaries
- Cultural degradation within organizations

Sun Tzu is far more concerned with indirect cost than direct cost, even when he does not label it as such.

When he warns against besieging cities, the issue is not just material expense—it is *what siege does to the army over time*: morale, discipline, patience, and vulnerability.

AWH principle: **direct cost is rarely fatal; indirect cost usually is**.

Visible Cost vs. Hidden Cost

Visible Cost

Visible costs are those acknowledged in advance:

- Budgets
- Timelines
- Headcount
- Stated risk

These are the costs decision-makers feel comfortable discussing because they can be defended, justified, and tracked.

Hidden Cost

Hidden costs are the primary source of strategic failure.

They include:

- Opportunity foregone
- Reputation risk not yet triggered
- Internal dissent suppressed rather than resolved
- Psychological commitment escalation
- Loss of bargaining power

Sun Tzu understands hidden cost intuitively:

> "If you lay siege to a town, you will exhaust your strength."

Exhaustion is not immediately visible. It accumulates quietly and reveals itself only when recovery is no longer possible.

AWH language is explicit: **hidden cost is cost you have not yet named, not cost that does not exist**.

Compounding Cost vs. Terminal Cost

This distinction is critical.

Compounding Cost

Compounding costs grow over time, often exponentially.

Examples include:

- Interest on debt
- Morale decay
- Reputational erosion
- Strategic distraction
- Cognitive commitment to failing paths

These costs worsen simply by remaining unresolved.

Sun Tzu warns against this when he condemns prolonged conflict. The danger is not the battle—it is the *accumulation.*

Terminal Cost

Terminal costs are one-time, finite, and bounded.

Examples include:

- A known financial loss
- A decisive exit
- A reputational hit that stabilizes afterward

Terminal costs can be painful but survivable. Compounding costs are often invisible until they are fatal.

AWH principle: **a large terminal cost is often preferable to a small compounding one**.

Sun Tzu's emphasis on swift resolution reflects this logic, not a desire for aggression.

Cost and Optionality

Optionality—the ability to choose among multiple futures—is the most valuable strategic asset.

Cost is dangerous because it collapses optionality.

Every resource spent, every position revealed, every tolerance tested reduces the number of future paths available.

Sun Tzu implicitly prioritizes optionality when he writes:

> "Do not press a desperate foe too hard."

Desperation eliminates options—for both sides. It forces terminal outcomes where maneuver once existed.

AWH reframes cost as **option destruction rate**.

The faster a decision destroys options, the more dangerous it is—regardless of upside.

Cost Asymmetry

Cost is not distributed evenly.

One of Sun Tzu's most important insights is that strategy is about shifting cost onto others while containing your own.

> "He who occupies the field of battle first and awaits
> his enemy is at ease; he who comes later and rushes
> into the fight is weary."

The weary side is paying higher cost per unit of action. Fatigue, confusion, and disorder are costs incurred simply by posture.

AWH principle: **the side paying less cost per decision gains compounding advantage**.

Cost Before Action, Not After

Modern systems often evaluate cost post-hoc. *The Art of War* evaluates cost *ex ante*.

Sun Tzu's repeated insistence on calculation before engagement reflects this:

> "The general who wins a battle makes many
> calculations in his temple before the battle is fought."

Calculation is cost analysis.

If cost cannot be calculated—even approximately—action is not bold. It is blind.

The Failure Mode: Winning That Destroys Future Optionality

This framework identifies a specific, recurring failure mode:

Winning that destroys future optionality.

This is one of the most dangerous illusions in modern strategy.

Examples include:

- Acquisitions that succeed financially but cripple flexibility
- Legal victories that provoke long-term retaliation
- Market wins that attract regulatory or competitive pressure
- Leadership decisions that "work" but fracture culture

Sun Tzu warns against hollow victories:

> "In war, then, let your great object be victory, not lengthy campaigns."

Victory here is not triumph—it is *closure without exhaustion*.

AWH language clarifies the point: **a win that narrows future choices is not a strategic success; it is deferred failure**.

Why Decision-Makers Underestimate Cost

Cost is underestimated because:

- It accumulates slowly
- It hides in second-order effects
- It conflicts with narratives of success
- It is emotionally inconvenient

Sun Tzu's system resists narrative thinking. It is procedural, not celebratory.

There are no victory speeches in *The Art of War*. There is only survival and advantage.

Cost as a Constraint, Not a Variable

Variables can be optimized. Constraints must be respected.

Cost is a constraint.

You cannot optimize away exhaustion, tolerance, or optionality loss. You can only choose *where* to incur them.

Sun Tzu's genius lies in forcing that choice early—before emotion, ego, or momentum take over.

Cost Discipline as Strategic Character

Throughout *The Art of War*, the most praised quality of commanders is not brilliance, courage, or creativity.

It is restraint.

> "He who is prudent and lies in wait for an enemy who is not, will be victorious."

Prudence is cost discipline.

AWH reframes character not as morality, but as **consistency in cost containment under pressure**.

Practical Cost Evaluation Questions

Before any decision, this framework requires explicit answers to the following:

1. What direct costs are unavoidable?
2. What indirect costs are likely but unacknowledged?
3. Which costs compound over time?
4. Which costs are terminal and bounded?
5. How does this decision reduce future optionality?
6. Who bears the cost now—and who bears it later?

If these questions cannot be answered, action is premature.

Cost Is the First Gate

Cost is evaluated first because it governs everything that follows:

- Information interpretation
- Timing decisions
- Risk tolerance
- Action sequencing

Sun Tzu understood this instinctively. AWH makes it explicit.

Closing Orientation

This chapter establishes **Cost** as the first and most unforgiving decision primitive.

Not because cost is the only thing that matters—but because it is the thing that silently determines how long anything else can matter.

Strategy does not fail because leaders lack ambition.
It fails because they misprice what ambition consumes.

The Art of War is not a manual for winning at all costs.

It is a system for **never paying costs you cannot survive**.

Everything that follows in this framework builds on that discipline.

Chapter 6

Risk

Introduction: Why Risk Is Always Misunderstood

Risk is one of the most abused words in modern decision-making.

It is treated as a percentage.
It is treated as a forecast.
It is treated as something that can be averaged, diversified, or "priced in."

This treatment is not merely incomplete—it is dangerous.

In **The Art of War**, risk is never reduced to probability. Sun Tzu does not ask how *likely* a loss is. He asks whether a loss, *if it occurs*, can be survived.

This distinction is foundational.

> **Risk is not the chance that something goes wrong.**
> **Risk is exposure to loss when it does.**

This chapter formalizes risk as the second decision primitive. It follows cost because risk is the **mechanism by which future cost becomes unavoidable**.

Where cost defines what you cannot afford to lose, risk defines how you might lose it—often without warning, often without drama, and almost always before you believe you are in danger.

Risk Is Exposure, Not Probability

Modern risk models obsess over likelihood.

They ask:

- How probable is this outcome?
- What are the odds?
- What is the expected value?

Sun Tzu does not think this way.

He assumes that **rare events happen**, and when they do, they dominate outcomes.

A low-probability ambush that annihilates an army matters more than a high-probability skirmish that costs little. A single catastrophic error outweighs dozens of minor successes.

Sun Tzu's thinking reflects this implicitly:

> "If you know yourself but not the enemy, for every victory gained you will also suffer a defeat."

This is not about frequency. It is about *exposure*. Partial blindness creates openings for catastrophic loss, regardless of how well things usually go.

AWH language is blunt: **probability comforts; exposure kills**.

Why Probability Thinking Fails in Strategy

Probability models assume repeatability.

Strategy rarely allows it.

Most strategic decisions are:

- One-time or infrequent
- Irreversible
- Highly asymmetric in outcome

There is no "average" acquisition, war, lawsuit, or leadership crisis. Each carries unique downside, and downside does not average out across attempts.

Sun Tzu never argues that generals should accept risk because it is unlikely to materialize. He argues they should **avoid exposure entirely where possible**.

> "Move not unless you see an advantage; use not your troops unless there is something to be gained."

This is not caution—it is exposure control.

Low-Probability, High-Cost Events Dominate Outcomes

Most strategic disasters come from events that were:

- Considered unlikely
- Poorly modeled
- Dismissed as edge cases
- Labeled "black swans" after the fact

Sun Tzu did not believe in black swans. He believed in **poor anticipation**.

Surprise, in his system, is not mysterious. It is the predictable result of unexamined exposure.

Ambushes, supply collapses, internal revolt, leadership betrayal—these are not random. They emerge from conditions that were tolerated because they were uncomfortable to confront.

AWH principle: **rare losses matter more than frequent gains**.

Risk Accumulates Quietly

One of the most dangerous properties of risk is that it accumulates without signaling.

You do not feel risk growing.

You feel momentum.
You feel confidence.
You feel validated.

Sun Tzu warns against this indirectly through his emphasis on
discipline and restraint. He knows that success breeds
complacency, and complacency widens exposure.

> "The general who is victorious makes few mistakes."

The implication is not perfection. It is *risk containment*. Mistakes
are minimized not by brilliance, but by limiting how much damage
any single mistake can cause.

Risk accumulates through:

- Repeated small compromises
- Overextension after success
- Tolerance of weak signals
- Normalization of deviation

Each compromise seems harmless. Together, they create fragility.

AWH language names this explicitly: **risk compounds in silence**.

The Difference Between Risk and Uncertainty

Risk is often conflated with uncertainty. They are not the same.

- **Uncertainty** is not knowing what will happen.
- **Risk** is being exposed to unacceptable loss if it does.

Sun Tzu accepts uncertainty as inevitable. He does not accept uncontrolled risk.

> "He who is prudent and lies in wait for an enemy who is not, will be victorious."

Waiting reduces exposure. It does not eliminate uncertainty.

AWH reframes the goal: **reduce exposure, not uncertainty**.

Risk and Irreversibility

The most dangerous risks are those tied to irreversible outcomes.

Examples include:

- Permanent capital loss
- Reputational destruction
- Loss of trust
- Legal or regulatory lock-in
- Strategic signaling that cannot be walked back

Sun Tzu repeatedly warns against irreversible commitment:

> "Do not press a desperate foe too hard."

Desperation collapses reversibility. It forces terminal outcomes where maneuver once existed.

AWH principle: **risk increases exponentially as reversibility decreases**.

Why Risk Is Ignored Until It Is Too Late

Risk is ignored because:

- It does not announce itself
- It conflicts with narratives of competence
- It threatens momentum
- It requires restraint, not action

Decision-makers often say, "We'll manage the risk later."

Sun Tzu would recognize this as folly.

By the time risk becomes visible, it has usually become cost.

Risk Is Not Symmetric

One of Sun Tzu's most important insights is that **risk does not affect all sides equally**.

The side with:

- Less flexibility
- Fewer resources
- Lower tolerance

- Weaker morale

Bears higher risk per action.

> "He who occupies the field first and awaits his enemy is at ease."

The weary side is not just tired—it is exposed. Time, fatigue, and pressure magnify risk asymmetrically.

AWH language: **risk follows weakness, not intention.**

The Illusion of Risk Transfer

Modern systems often claim to "transfer" risk—through insurance, contracts, delegation, or diversification.

Some risk can be shifted. Core risk cannot.

Sun Tzu never assumes risk can be outsourced. Commanders bear ultimate exposure regardless of intermediaries.

> "The general is the bulwark of the State."

This is not praise. It is liability assignment.

AWH principle: **if you cannot absorb the downside, you still own the risk—even if someone else executes the action.**

Risk and Ego

Ego magnifies risk more reliably than ignorance.

Sun Tzu explicitly warns against ego-driven exposure:

> "The general who is choleric and quick-tempered may
> be provoked by insults."

Provocation creates emotional urgency. Urgency collapses risk
discipline.

Most catastrophic risks are taken not because they are
misunderstood, but because they are **rationalized**.

AWH language is unforgiving: **ego is a risk multiplier**.

Risk Mapping Before Action

This framework requires risk to be mapped explicitly before any
decision.

Not in probabilities, but in exposure categories:

1. What losses are possible?
2. Which losses are irreversible?
3. How much of that loss can be absorbed?
4. What early signals indicate escalation?
5. What exits exist if conditions deteriorate?

Sun Tzu's insistence on calculation before engagement reflects this logic.

> "The general who loses a battle makes but few calculations beforehand."

Failure is not bad luck. It is unexamined exposure.

Risk and Compounding

Risk compounds when:

- Multiple exposures align
- Time magnifies fragility
- Success encourages overreach

A series of small, tolerable risks can combine into a single intolerable one.

Sun Tzu's aversion to prolonged campaigns reflects this understanding. Each extension adds exposure without proportional gain.

AWH principle: **compounded risk collapses suddenly, not gradually**.

Risk Versus Reward Asymmetry

One of the most dangerous miscalculations is asymmetric risk-reward.

When:

- Upside is capped
- Downside is uncapped

No probability justifies action.

Sun Tzu never advocates such positions.

"There are roads which must not be followed."

Some paths are forbidden not because they never work, but because when they fail, they destroy everything.

AWH language is explicit: **no upside justifies existential exposure**.

The Rule Formalized

Risk unmanaged becomes cost realized.

This is not metaphorical.

Every unmanaged exposure eventually expresses itself as:

- Loss

- Constraint
- Forced action

Risk does not disappear. It converts.

Sun Tzu's entire system is designed to prevent this conversion by reducing exposure before it is tested.

Strategic Restraint as Risk Control

Restraint is often misinterpreted as fear.

Sun Tzu treats it as intelligence.

> "He who knows when he can fight and when he cannot will be victorious."

Knowing when you cannot fight is risk awareness.

AWH reframes restraint as **preemptive risk mitigation**, not hesitation.

When Risk Must Be Taken

This chapter does not argue for zero risk.

Risk is unavoidable.

The discipline lies in choosing *which* risks to bear, and *when*.

Acceptable risk has four properties:

- Loss is survivable
- Exposure is bounded
- Reversibility exists
- Timing favors you

Sun Tzu accepts risk only under these conditions.

Why Most Strategic Systems Fail on Risk

They:

- Model probability instead of exposure
- Ignore irreversibility
- Confuse confidence with safety
- Reward boldness over survivability

The Art of War avoids these traps by treating risk as structural, not statistical.

Closing Orientation

Risk is not the enemy of strategy.

Unmanaged risk is.

This chapter establishes risk as a decision primitive because it is the **bridge between intent and catastrophe**.

Cost defines what you cannot lose.
Risk defines how you might lose it.

Ignore risk, and cost will eventually assert itself—without warning, without negotiation, and without mercy.

Sun Tzu understood this.

Ancient Wisdom Hacks makes it explicit.

The strategist does not ask, *How likely is failure?*

He asks:

- If failure occurs, can we survive it?
- If not, why are we exposed?

Until those questions are answered, action is not strategy.

It is gambling under pressure.

Chapter 7

Timing

Introduction: Why Timing Is the Hidden Axis of All Strategy

Most strategic failure is explained incorrectly.

After the fact, leaders say:

- "We moved too slowly."
- "We missed the window."
- "We should have acted sooner."

Less often do they admit the real error:
we acted at the wrong time.

Timing is not speed.
Timing is not urgency.
Timing is not decisiveness.

Timing is **alignment between action and structural reality**.

In **The Art of War**, timing is never treated as a secondary consideration. It is not something layered onto a good plan. It *is* the plan.

Sun Tzu does not ask whether an action is bold, clever, or efficient. He asks whether the *moment* is correct.

> "He will win who knows when to fight and when not to fight."

This sentence contains an entire strategic worldview. Victory does not come from action alone. It comes from *correctly synchronized* action.

This chapter formalizes **Timing** as a decision primitive: an irreducible component that governs whether cost, risk, information, and action work together—or collapse into exposure.

Timing Is Not Linear

Modern thinking treats time as linear and uniform:

- Early is good.
- Late is bad.
- Faster is better.

This model is wrong.

Time is **nonlinear and asymmetric**. Its effect depends entirely on posture, preparation, and relative position.

The same action can be:

- Premature at one moment
- Catastrophic at another

- Decisive at a third

Sun Tzu never assumes that acting sooner is superior. He assumes that acting *at the correct moment* is everything.

AWH language is precise here:

> **Timing is not about when something happens.
> It is about when it becomes permissible.**

Early Timing: The Cost of Premature Action

Early action is often praised as bold leadership.

In reality, it is one of the most common failure modes.

Early action occurs when:

- Information has not stabilized
- Costs are still hidden
- Risk exposure is unclear
- Structure is unprepared

Sun Tzu warns against premature engagement repeatedly, though often indirectly:

> "Move not unless you see an advantage; use not your troops unless there is something to be gained."

Advantage is not desire. It is not vision. It is not confidence.

Advantage is **structural readiness**.

Early action creates three dangerous conditions:

1. **Forced commitment before understanding**
2. **Acceleration of hidden cost**
3. **Loss of strategic surprise**

AWH principle: **early action spends optionality before it produces leverage**.

The Illusion of "Getting Ahead"

Many decision-makers justify early action with the language of initiative:

- "First-mover advantage"
- "Setting the narrative"
- "Controlling the board"

Sun Tzu would reject this framing outright.

Initiative without structure is not advantage—it is exposure.

To act early is to reveal intent, position, and capability before necessity demands it. This allows opponents, markets, or circumstances to adapt.

> "When able to attack, we must seem unable; when using our forces, we must seem inactive."

This is not deception for drama's sake. It is **timing discipline**.

Early action collapses ambiguity in favor of the other side.

Late Timing: The Cost of Decay

If early action is exposure, late action is erosion.

Late timing occurs when:

- Costs have already accumulated
- Tolerance has degraded
- Opponents have repositioned
- Optionality has narrowed

Sun Tzu condemns prolonged indecision not because it lacks courage, but because it consumes strength.

> "There is no instance of a nation benefiting from prolonged warfare."

The danger of lateness is not delay itself—it is **delay without positional improvement**.

AWH language is explicit:

Waiting that improves position is patience.
Waiting that weakens position is decay.

Late action often feels forced. It lacks flexibility. It is executed under pressure rather than choice.

At that point, timing is no longer strategic—it is reactive.

Correct Timing: The Only Moment That Matters

Correct timing is neither early nor late.

It is **the moment when structure, information, cost, and risk align favorably enough that action reduces exposure instead of increasing it**.

Sun Tzu describes this moment obliquely but consistently:

> "Victorious warriors win first and then go to war, while defeated warriors go to war first and then seek to win."

"Winning first" is not metaphorical. It means:

- Cost is contained
- Risk is bounded
- Information is sufficient
- Posture favors you

Only then does action become decisive.

AWH principle: **correct timing feels anticlimactic, not dramatic.**

When timing is right, action appears easy—not because it is simple, but because resistance has already been structurally reduced.

Timing as a Force Multiplier

When timing is correct, effort multiplies.

A small force achieves disproportionate effect.
A modest decision produces outsized outcome.
Minimal exposure yields significant gain.

Sun Tzu understood this deeply:

> "In war, then, let your great object be victory, not
> lengthy campaigns."

Victory achieved at the correct time ends conflict quickly. Victory pursued at the wrong time prolongs it.

AWH reframes this as **efficiency of consequence**: how much result is produced per unit of cost and risk.

Correct timing maximizes this ratio.

Timing as a Risk Reducer

One of the least understood functions of timing is **risk reduction**.

Most people assume risk must be accepted to act. In reality, risk is often reduced *by waiting*—if waiting improves posture.

Sun Tzu's emphasis on preparation reflects this:

> "The general who wins a battle makes many
> calculations in his temple before the battle is fought."

Calculation takes time.
Alignment takes time.
Risk mitigation takes time.

Correct timing allows:

- Fragile assumptions to break safely
- Weak signals to clarify
- Opponent mistakes to surface

AWH language: **timing converts uncertainty into manageable exposure**.

Why Fast Action Is So Often Misread as Strategic Action

Speed is visible. Timing is invisible.

Speed can be applauded. Timing can rarely be proven in advance.

This creates a cultural bias toward fast action—even when it is strategically inferior.

Sun Tzu never praises speed alone. When he does reference speed, it is conditional:

"Let your rapidity be that of the wind."

Rapidity follows preparation. It does not replace it.

Fast action without timing produces:

- Overcommitment
- Escalation traps
- Irreversible exposure

AWH rule is blunt:

Fast action is only strategic if it occurs at the correct time.

Otherwise, it is simply accelerated error.

The Misread: Fast Action ≠ Strategic Action

This chapter explicitly rejects one of the most damaging modern myths:

Fast action ≠ strategic action

Strategic action:

- Reduces future cost

- Narrows opponent options
- Preserves optionality
- Improves leverage

Fast action may do none of these.

Sun Tzu's system privileges **outcomes over optics**. He is unconcerned with how action appears. He is concerned with whether it works.

AWH language aligns with this discipline.

Timing and Information Maturity

Information does not become perfect with time—but it often becomes *useful*.

Correct timing depends on understanding:

- Which uncertainties matter
- Which will resolve naturally
- Which will not

Sun Tzu's emphasis on intelligence is not about knowing everything—it is about knowing *enough at the right moment*.

> "Spies are a most important element in war."

Information gathered too early is speculative. Information gathered too late is obsolete.

Timing determines whether information clarifies or misleads.

Timing and Opponent Error

One of the most underutilized strategic advantages is allowing others to move first—*when their movement increases their exposure.*

Sun Tzu legitimizes this:

> "If the enemy is secure at all points, be prepared for him. If he is in superior strength, evade him."

Evading is not retreat. It is **waiting for misalignment**.

Correct timing often involves restraint until others create openings for you.

AWH reframes this as **error harvesting**: allowing time to surface opponent mistakes rather than forcing confrontation.

Timing and Emotional Discipline

Emotions distort timing more reliably than lack of intelligence.

Anger accelerates action.
Fear delays action.
Pride misreads moments.

Sun Tzu identifies these dangers clearly:

> "The general who is choleric and quick-tempered may
> be provoked by insults."

Provocation creates false urgency. False urgency destroys timing.

AWH language is clear:

> **Urgency is an emotional state.**
> **Timing is a structural condition.**

Confusing the two guarantees failure.

Timing and Optionality Preservation

Correct timing preserves exit paths.

Early action closes options prematurely.
Late action forces commitment.
Correct timing keeps multiple futures alive until choice becomes
necessary.

Sun Tzu's caution against pressing desperate foes reflects this:

> "Do not press a desperate foe too hard."

Desperation collapses timing. It forces terminal outcomes.

AWH principle: **good timing delays irreversibility as long as
possible**.

Timing Across Strategic Domains

Timing applies universally:

- **Business**: entering markets after validation but before saturation
- **Negotiation**: making offers after leverage is established
- **Conflict**: engaging after morale and logistics favor you
- **Leadership**: intervening before decay but after signal clarity

The domain changes. The principle does not.

The Timing Diagnostic

Before action, this framework requires explicit answers to:

1. Is acting now cheaper or more expensive than acting later?
2. Does time favor our position or the opponent's?
3. What information will improve with delay?
4. What costs will compound with delay?
5. What risks are reduced by waiting—and which increase?

If these cannot be answered, timing is not understood.

Why Timing Cannot Be Delegated

Timing is a leadership responsibility.

Execution can be delegated.
Analysis can be delegated.
Timing cannot.

Sun Tzu assigns this burden squarely to the commander:

> "The general is the bulwark of the State."

Timing errors cascade downward. No amount of execution excellence can correct them.

AWH language: **a well-executed mistake is still a mistake**.

Timing as the Integrator of All Primitives

Timing integrates:

- Cost
- Risk
- Information
- Action

Without correct timing, each of these primitives works against the others.

With correct timing, they reinforce one another.

This is why timing appears throughout *The Art of War* rather than in a single section. It is not a tactic. It is a governing principle.

Closing Orientation

This chapter establishes **Timing** as a decisive primitive—not because it replaces cost, risk, or information, but because it governs how they interact.

Early action exposes you.
Late action traps you.
Correct timing liberates you.

Sun Tzu did not win by being fast.
He won by being *right in time*.

Ancient Wisdom Hacks makes this explicit:

> **Strategy is not about moving first.**
> **It is about moving when movement becomes unavoidable for the other side—and optional for you.**

Until timing is understood at this level, action is not strategic.

It is merely motion under pressure.

Chapter 8

Preparation

Introduction: Why Preparation Is Misunderstood

Preparation is routinely underestimated because it produces no visible outcome.

It does not announce itself.
It does not generate applause.
It does not feel decisive.

In most modern environments, preparation is mistaken for hesitation, overthinking, or lack of confidence. Action is celebrated. Movement is rewarded. Visibility is equated with progress.

The Art of War rejects this entire value system.

Sun Tzu treats preparation not as a preliminary step, but as the *primary locus of strategy*. Action is merely the final expression of work already completed.

> "Victorious warriors win first and then go to war, while defeated warriors go to war first and then seek to win."

This line is not poetic. It is procedural.

This chapter formalizes **Preparation** as a decision primitive—not because it precedes action chronologically, but because it determines whether action will be necessary, survivable, or even visible at all.

Preparation Is Where Strategy Actually Occurs

Most people believe strategy happens at the moment of decision.

It does not.

By the time a decision feels urgent, the strategy has already failed or succeeded—quietly, incrementally, and often invisibly.

Sun Tzu's system assumes this implicitly. He does not describe generals improvising under fire. He describes them calculating, aligning, provisioning, and positioning *before* engagement.

> "The general who wins a battle makes many
> calculations in his temple before the battle is fought."

Calculations are preparation.
Temples are private.
Battles are public.

AWH language is direct: **what happens in public is determined by what was done in private**.

Preparation Reduces Decision Complexity

One of the most important—and least appreciated—functions of preparation is **complexity reduction**.

Unprepared decisions feel overwhelming because too many variables are live at once:

- Cost is unclear
- Risk is entangled
- Information is ambiguous
- Timing feels urgent
- Options are poorly defined

Preparation does not eliminate complexity. It *organizes it.*

Sun Tzu never attempts to control every variable. He isolates the ones that matter and neutralizes the rest.

> "He who knows the enemy and knows himself will not
> be endangered in a hundred engagements."

Knowing does not mean memorizing facts. It means **structuring awareness** so that irrelevant uncertainty does not dominate judgment.

AWH reframes preparation as **pre-decision pruning**: eliminating paths, risks, and assumptions *before* they reach the point of action.

Why Unprepared Decisions Feel Dramatic

Drama is a symptom of poor preparation.

When preparation is weak:

- Decisions feel urgent
- Stakes feel existential
- Emotions spike
- Errors feel irreversible

This is not because the situation is inherently dramatic. It is because uncertainty has been allowed to accumulate unchecked.

Sun Tzu's writing is notably undramatic for a treatise on war. There are no heroic arcs. No climactic speeches. No emotional language.

That restraint is intentional.

Prepared strategy feels calm because exposure has already been reduced.

AWH language is explicit:

> **If a decision feels dramatic, preparation has failed somewhere upstream.**

Preparation Converts Uncertainty Into Bounded Risk

Uncertainty cannot be eliminated.

Sun Tzu accepts this fully. He never promises clarity. What he promises is *containment*.

Preparation works by converting open-ended uncertainty into **bounded risk**—risk that is:

- Identified
- Limited
- Absorbable

This conversion happens through:

- Scenario mapping
- Cost classification
- Exit definition
- Resource staging
- Information filtering

Sun Tzu's emphasis on logistics, discipline, and intelligence reflects this conversion process.

> "The clever combatant looks to the effect of combined energy, and does not require too much from individuals."

Combined energy is preparation. It replaces improvisation with structure.

AWH reframes this as **uncertainty compression**: narrowing the range of outcomes so that none are catastrophic.

Preparation Is Invisible Leverage

One of the most dangerous misconceptions in modern strategy is that leverage must be visible to be real.

Sun Tzu disagrees.

He treats leverage as something created quietly, often through *inaction*.

> "Appear weak when you are strong, and strong when you are weak."

This is not deception for deception's sake. It is preparation that alters perception and therefore behavior.

Prepared positions exert pressure without movement. They force others to hesitate, misjudge, or overcommit.

AWH language defines invisible leverage as **structural advantage that does not require enforcement**.

Examples include:

- Financial runway that allows patience
- Legal positioning that deters escalation
- Information asymmetry that shapes negotiation
- Operational readiness that makes speed optional

None of these announce themselves. All of them shape outcomes.

Why Preparation Is Devalued

Preparation is devalued because:

- It is hard to measure
- It does not create immediate wins
- It delays visible action
- It threatens ego-driven narratives

Prepared leaders do not look heroic. They look cautious, methodical, and unhurried.

Sun Tzu praises exactly these qualities.

> "The general who is skilled in defense hides in the most secret recesses of the earth."

Hiding here is not fear. It is **strategic invisibility**—the hallmark of preparation.

AWH language is blunt: **preparation offends cultures addicted to momentum**.

Preparation and Cost Containment

Preparation is the primary mechanism for controlling cost.

Unprepared action pays full price for every mistake. Prepared action absorbs error cheaply.

Sun Tzu repeatedly warns against actions that consume resources unnecessarily:

> "If you lay siege to a town, you will exhaust your strength."

Why? Because siege represents failure of preparation. It is what happens when positioning, intelligence, and timing were insufficient to avoid direct confrontation.

AWH principle: **the better the preparation, the less cost action requires**.

Preparation and Risk Suppression

Risk does not disappear through courage. It disappears through preparation.

Prepared systems:

- Fail gracefully
- Detect problems early
- Preserve reversibility
- Avoid single points of collapse

Sun Tzu's emphasis on discipline reflects this. Discipline is not obedience—it is **predictability under pressure**.

"If words of command are not clear and distinct, if orders are not thoroughly understood, the general is to blame."

Clarity is preparation. Confusion is risk.

AWH language frames preparation as **risk damping**—reducing the amplitude of negative outcomes when things go wrong.

Preparation Versus Planning

Preparation is often confused with planning. They are not the same.

- **Planning** assumes stability
- **Preparation** assumes disruption

Plans are linear. Preparation is modular.

Sun Tzu rarely outlines fixed plans. He outlines *principles* that allow adaptation.

"In the midst of chaos, there is also opportunity."

Opportunity exists only for those who are prepared to exploit it.

AWH language distinguishes clearly:

Plans break. Preparation adapts.

Preparation and Timing Discipline

Preparation creates timing freedom.

Unprepared actors are forced to act when pressure peaks. Prepared actors choose when to move.

Sun Tzu's preference for waiting reflects this:

> "He who is prudent and lies in wait for an enemy who is not, will be victorious."

Waiting without preparation is decay. Waiting *with* preparation is leverage.

AWH principle: **preparation turns time into an ally**.

Preparation and Information Filtering

Preparation determines how information is interpreted.

Unprepared actors treat every signal as urgent. Prepared actors know which signals matter.

Sun Tzu's emphasis on intelligence is inseparable from preparation:

> "Spies are a most important element in war."

Intelligence without preparation overwhelms. Intelligence with preparation clarifies.

AWH language frames this as **interpretive readiness**—the ability
to process incomplete information without panic.

Preparation and Organizational Stability

In organizations, preparation manifests as:

- Clear authority lines
- Defined escalation thresholds
- Pre-agreed decision rules
- Resource buffers

Sun Tzu understands the danger of ambiguity:

> "If soldiers are punished before they have grown
> attached to you, they will not prove submissive."

Attachment here is trust. Trust is built through preparation, not
reaction.

AWH principle: **prepared organizations absorb shock;
unprepared ones amplify it**.

Why Prepared Decisions Feel Boring

Prepared decisions rarely feel exciting.

They are:

- Methodical
- Predictable
- Low-drama
- Often anticlimactic

This is not a flaw. It is the point.

Sun Tzu does not glorify intensity. He glorifies *effectiveness*.

> "To subdue the enemy without fighting is the acme of skill."

No drama. No spectacle. Just outcome.

AWH insight is explicit:

> **Prepared decisions feel boring.**
> **That is their strength.**

Boredom indicates that uncertainty has already been resolved where it matters.

The Emotional Trap of Improvisation

Improvisation is often mistaken for adaptability.

In reality, improvisation under pressure is usually **compensating for missing preparation**.

Sun Tzu allows flexibility, but only on a prepared foundation:

> "Water shapes its course according to the nature of
> the ground over which it flows."

Water is flexible because it is unconstrained by structure—not because it lacks one. Its structure is intrinsic.

AWH language reframes this: **true flexibility is pre-built, not improvised**.

Preparation as Ethical Discipline

There is an ethical dimension to preparation that is often ignored.

Unprepared decisions shift cost onto others:

- Teams
- Families
- Stakeholders
- Institutions

Sun Tzu's insistence on preparation is partly moral, though never sentimental.

> "The general is the bulwark of the State."

Failure of preparation is failure of responsibility.

AWH language is unambiguous: **those who bear authority owe preparation to those who bear consequence**.

The Preparation Checklist (Framework Standard)

Before action, this framework requires explicit confirmation that:

1. Costs have been classified and bounded
2. Risks have been mapped and reduced
3. Information gaps are understood
4. Timing favors action more than delay
5. Exit conditions exist and are viable
6. Authority and execution are aligned

If these conditions are not met, the decision is not ready.

Why Preparation Cannot Be Rushed

Preparation resists compression.

It requires:

- Observation over time
- Stress-testing assumptions
- Allowing weak signals to emerge

Sun Tzu never advocates rushing preparation. He advocates rushing *execution* after preparation is complete.

> "Let your rapidity be that of the wind."

Rapidity comes last.

AWH language reinforces this ordering:

Preparation is slow so that execution can be fast.

Preparation as the Silent Advantage

Prepared actors are often underestimated.

They do not signal urgency.
They do not telegraph intent.
They do not rush to be seen.

Sun Tzu treats this as an advantage, not a liability.

> "He who exercises no forethought but makes light of
> his opponents is sure to be captured by them."

Forethought is preparation.

Closing Orientation

This chapter establishes **Preparation** as a decision primitive not
because it is optional, but because it is *decisive without being
visible*.

Preparation:

- Reduces complexity

- Converts uncertainty into bounded risk
- Creates invisible leverage
- Preserves timing freedom

And most importantly, it makes decisions boring.

Not because they are trivial—but because the danger has already been removed.

Sun Tzu did not win by reacting well under pressure.
He won by **ensuring pressure never arrived unexpectedly**.

Ancient Wisdom Hacks makes this explicit:

> **If a decision feels exciting, it is probably late.**
> **If it feels boring, it is probably ready.**

That is not weakness.

That is preparation doing its job.

Chapter 9

Visibility

Introduction: The Cost of Being Seen

Modern strategy is obsessed with visibility.

Be visible.
Be loud.
Signal strength.
Control the narrative.

This obsession is not accidental. Visibility feels like power. It produces validation, attention, and the illusion of control. In competitive environments—business, politics, media, leadership—visibility is often treated as proof of relevance.

The Art of War rejects this instinct almost entirely.

Sun Tzu does not equate being seen with being strong. He equates being seen with being *targetable*.

Visibility attracts attention.
Attention attracts resistance.
Resistance attracts counteraction.

This chapter formalizes **Visibility** as a decision primitive—an irreducible element that must be evaluated before action, communication, or movement. Visibility is not neutral. It reshapes cost, risk, timing, and optionality the moment it increases.

The central principle of this chapter is uncompromising:

Visibility is a liability unless deliberately traded.

Visibility Is Not Free

Every increase in visibility carries cost.

This cost is rarely immediate. That is why it is underestimated.

Visibility costs include:

- Loss of ambiguity
- Increased scrutiny
- Accelerated opposition
- Reduced maneuver space
- Forced signaling commitments

Sun Tzu never treats visibility casually. His entire strategic posture is built around **controlled appearance**.

> "When able to attack, we must seem unable; when using our forces, we must seem inactive."

This is not theatrical deception. It is **exposure management**.

AWH language is precise: **what you reveal, you lose control over**.

Visibility Attracts Attention, Resistance, and Counteraction

Visibility does not merely inform others of your presence. It *invites response*.

Once visible, you are no longer operating in a unilateral decision space. You are operating in a reactive system.

Sun Tzu understands this deeply. He assumes that every visible action produces adaptation by others:

> "If the enemy leaves a door open, you must rush in."

Visibility creates doors—for others.

The more visible your intent, position, or strength:

- The faster others adapt
- The more resistance you encounter
- The more countermeasures are deployed

AWH principle: **visibility accelerates the opponent's decision cycle, not yours**.

Why Modern Systems Overvalue Visibility

Visibility is overvalued because it:

- Signals confidence
- Satisfies ego
- Produces social proof
- Feels like progress

None of these are strategic outcomes.

Sun Tzu never praises confidence displays. He praises *effectiveness*.

> "He who knows when he can fight and when he cannot will be victorious."

Knowing when *not* to be seen is embedded in this wisdom.

AWH language is blunt: **confidence that requires visibility is insecurity wearing armor**.

Transparency Increases Vulnerability

Transparency is often framed as a moral or cultural good. In internal systems, it can build trust. In adversarial environments, it increases vulnerability.

Sun Tzu does not confuse ethics with exposure. He is not dishonest—but he is not transparent.

> "All warfare is based on deception."

This line is frequently misunderstood as endorsement of lying. It is not. It is recognition that **full disclosure in adversarial contexts is self-harm**.

Transparency exposes:

- Intent
- Capability
- Timing
- Constraints

Each exposure narrows optionality.

AWH reframes transparency as **context-dependent disclosure**, not a universal virtue.

Visibility and Information Asymmetry

Information asymmetry is a source of power. Visibility collapses it.

The more others know about:

- Your resources
- Your priorities
- Your constraints

The more accurately they can price risk against you.

Sun Tzu's emphasis on secrecy reflects this:

> "Be subtle! Be subtle! And use your spies for every kind of business."

Subtlety is not dishonesty. It is **information discipline**.

AWH principle: **what others do not know about you cannot be used against you**.

Obscurity Preserves Optionality

Optionality—the ability to choose among multiple futures—depends on ambiguity.

Visibility resolves ambiguity.
Obscurity preserves it.

Sun Tzu repeatedly emphasizes the value of remaining unreadable:

> "The general who is skilled in defense hides in the most secret recesses of the earth."

Hiding here is strategic obscurity, not retreat.

Obscurity allows:

- Delayed commitment

- Flexible response
- Asymmetric patience
- Error correction without penalty

AWH language defines obscurity as **freedom from forced reaction**.

Visibility Collapses Timing Advantage

Visibility compresses time.

Once visible:

- Others begin planning against you
- Windows close faster
- Pressure increases

Sun Tzu's preference for waiting reflects this:

> "He who is prudent and lies in wait for an enemy who
> is not, will be victorious."

Waiting requires obscurity. Visibility turns waiting into vulnerability.

AWH principle: **visibility forces timing decisions before they are ready**.

The Cost of Being Interpreted

Visibility is not just about being seen—it is about being interpreted.

Interpretation is uncontrolled.

Once visible, others assign motives, exaggerate threats, misread signals, and respond to narratives you did not intend.

Sun Tzu understands this danger:

> "Appear weak when you are strong, and strong when you are weak."

This is not manipulation. It is **interpretation management**.

AWH language: **you do not control how visibility is understood—only whether it exists**.

Visibility and Ego

Ego craves recognition. Strategy avoids it.

Many visibility decisions are not strategic; they are psychological:

- Announcing too early
- Signaling strength unnecessarily
- Publicly committing to paths prematurely

Sun Tzu explicitly warns against ego-driven exposure:

"The general who is choleric and quick-tempered may
be provoked by insults."

Provocation works only when visibility creates emotional
response.

AWH principle: **ego converts visibility into liability faster than
any opponent**.

Visibility as a Trigger for Escalation

Escalation often begins not with action, but with visibility.

Once visible:

- Others feel compelled to respond
- Neutral parties choose sides
- Dormant opposition activates

Sun Tzu avoids escalation whenever possible:

"To fight and conquer in all your battles is not supreme
excellence; supreme excellence consists in breaking
the enemy's resistance without fighting."

Breaking resistance often means never triggering it.

AWH reframes this as **escalation avoidance through obscurity**.

Visibility and Resource Drain

Visibility consumes resources indirectly.

Being seen requires:

- Justification
- Defense
- Narrative management
- Continuous signaling

These drain attention and energy.

Sun Tzu never describes generals managing optics. He describes them managing logistics, morale, and positioning.

AWH language is explicit: **what you spend explaining cannot be spent maneuvering**.

The Myth of "Owning the Narrative"

Modern strategy culture emphasizes narrative control.

Sun Tzu does not.

Narratives are unstable. They provoke reaction. They require constant reinforcement.

Structural advantage does not.

AWH principle: **if your strategy depends on narrative dominance, it is fragile**.

When Visibility Becomes Necessary

This chapter does not argue for permanent invisibility.

Visibility can be useful—but only when deliberately traded for something concrete.

Visibility is acceptable when:

- Leverage has already been secured
- Risk is bounded
- Cost is contained
- Timing favors exposure

Sun Tzu allows visibility *after* advantage is established:

> "Let your rapidity be that of the wind."

Speed and visibility are acceptable when opposition can no longer adapt meaningfully.

Visibility as a Strategic Trade

Visibility is not inherently bad. It is **expensive**.

Like any expensive asset, it should be used sparingly and intentionally.

AWH language frames this clearly:

Visibility should be spent, not indulged.

Before increasing visibility, the framework requires explicit answers:

1. What advantage does visibility create?
2. What resistance will it trigger?
3. What optionality does it destroy?
4. Can we absorb the resulting attention?
5. Is obscurity still available as an alternative?

If these questions cannot be answered, visibility is premature.

Visibility and Commitment Lock-In

Visibility locks you into paths.

Public commitments reduce flexibility. They turn reconsideration into reputational cost.

Sun Tzu avoids public commitment entirely. His system is private, procedural, and adaptive.

AWH principle: **commitment should follow success, not precede it**.

Visibility in Modern Domains

Visibility applies across domains:

- **Business**: premature announcements attract competition
- **Negotiation**: visible desperation weakens leverage
- **Leadership**: public certainty limits adaptation
- **Conflict**: visible intent invites preemption

The pattern is consistent: visibility narrows the decision space.

The Strategic Value of Silence

Silence is not emptiness. It is capacity.

Sun Tzu never fills silence with explanation. He allows ambiguity to work on his behalf.

> "He who exercises no forethought but makes light of his opponents is sure to be captured by them."

Forethought includes knowing when *not* to speak or act.

AWH language reframes silence as **strategic bandwidth**.

Visibility and Failure Amplification

When visible actors fail, failure is amplified.

Mistakes become signals. Weakness becomes contagious. Recovery becomes harder.

Sun Tzu avoids this by avoiding exposure until outcomes are secured.

AWH principle: **visibility magnifies both success and failure—choose when amplification is safe**.

The Principle Restated

Visibility is a liability unless deliberately traded.

This is not cynicism. It is realism.

Visibility:

- Accelerates opposition
- Reduces optionality
- Increases risk
- Consumes resources

Obscurity:

- Preserves timing
- Protects leverage

- Allows adaptation
- Contains cost

Closing Orientation

This chapter establishes **Visibility** as a decision primitive because
it silently governs how others respond to you.

Sun Tzu did not win by being seen.
He won by being *unavoidable*—often only at the moment
resistance was futile.

Ancient Wisdom Hacks makes the discipline explicit:

> **Do not ask, "Should we be seen?"**
> **Ask, "What does being seen cost us—and what**
> **do we receive in return?"**

Until visibility is treated as a liability to be managed rather than a
virtue to be pursued, strategy will remain fragile.

The unseen often decide outcomes.

Chapter 10

Restraint

Introduction: The Discipline That Looks Like Weakness

Restraint is the most misunderstood discipline in strategy.

It is mistaken for fear.
It is dismissed as indecision.
It is confused with passivity or lack of ambition.

In environments that reward visibility, speed, and assertion, restraint appears countercultural—sometimes even irresponsible. Leaders are praised for acting, responding, intervening, and "doing something." Silence is suspicious. Delay is criticized. Non-action is framed as failure.

The Art of War rejects this bias completely.

Sun Tzu does not equate strength with action. He equates strength with **control**. And control, more often than not, is expressed through restraint.

> "He who knows when he can fight and when he cannot, will be victorious."

This is not advice about courage. It is a statement about *discipline*. Knowing when *not* to act is not avoidance—it is mastery of cost, risk, timing, and visibility.

This chapter formalizes **Restraint** as a decision primitive. Not as an ethical preference, and not as a personality trait—but as an **active strategic posture** that preserves resources, prevents escalation, and protects optionality.

The core truth that governs this chapter is simple, uncomfortable, and repeatedly validated by history:

The best action is often the one not taken.

Restraint Is Not Inaction

The first error to correct is definitional.

Restraint is not doing nothing.
Restraint is doing *less than you could* in order to preserve what matters more.

In *The Art of War*, restraint is everywhere, though it is rarely named explicitly. Sun Tzu's system is built around avoidance: avoiding direct conflict, avoiding prolonged campaigns, avoiding siege, avoiding desperation, avoiding unnecessary exposure.

> "To fight and conquer in all your battles is not supreme excellence; supreme excellence consists in breaking the enemy's resistance without fighting."

This line is often quoted and rarely understood.

Sun Tzu is not advocating peace. He is advocating **outcome without cost**. He is identifying restraint as the mechanism by which force becomes unnecessary.

AWH language is explicit:

> **Restraint is action taken at the level of structure rather than movement.**

It is what you do *before* force becomes required.

Restraint Preserves Resources

Every action consumes resources.

Some are obvious:

- Money
- Time
- Personnel
- Energy

Others are less visible:

- Attention
- Credibility
- Morale
- Strategic flexibility

Restraint preserves all of them.

Sun Tzu's repeated warnings against prolonged warfare are not moral objections. They are resource calculations.

> "There is no instance of a nation benefiting from prolonged warfare."

Prolongation is what happens when restraint fails early. When leaders act too often, too visibly, or too aggressively, they spend resources to solve problems that restraint would have dissolved.

AWH reframes this clearly:

> **Every action has a carrying cost.**
> **Restraint is how you stop paying rent on unnecessary problems.**

Restraint Prevents Escalation

Escalation is one of the most dangerous dynamics in strategy.

It rarely begins intentionally.
It accelerates quickly.
It is difficult to reverse.

Most escalation begins not with decisive action, but with *unnecessary response*.

Sun Tzu is acutely aware of this danger:

"The general who is choleric and quick-tempered may
be provoked by insults."

Provocation works only when restraint is absent. Insults,
challenges, and perceived slights are escalation traps designed to
force premature action.

Restraint interrupts this process.

AWH language is precise:

**Restraint denies the opponent the reaction they
are trying to provoke.**

Without reaction, escalation stalls. Without escalation, cost
remains contained.

Restraint as an Active Posture

Restraint is not passive waiting.

Passive waiting is decay.
Active restraint is positioning.

Sun Tzu makes this distinction repeatedly, though indirectly:

"He who is prudent and lies in wait for an enemy who
is not, will be victorious."

"Lying in wait" is not idleness. It is **prepared stillness**. It assumes
readiness, awareness, and capacity—held in reserve.

AWH reframes this distinction clearly:

- **Passivity**: waiting because you cannot act
- **Restraint**: not acting because you do not need to

Only the second preserves leverage.

Why Restraint Feels Uncomfortable

Restraint creates psychological tension.

Action relieves anxiety.
Restraint sustains it.

Many leaders act not because action is correct, but because inaction is uncomfortable. Silence feels like exposure. Waiting feels like weakness. Not responding feels like loss of control.

Sun Tzu understands this weakness and designs his system to counter it. His writing is deliberately unemotional. He removes ego, honor, and pride from decision-making.

> "If your opponent is of choleric temper, seek to irritate him."

This only works when restraint is absent.

AWH language is blunt:

> **Most bad decisions are made to relieve emotional pressure, not strategic necessity.**

Restraint is the discipline of refusing that relief.

Restraint and Optionality

Optionality—the ability to choose among multiple futures—is preserved by restraint.

Every action collapses options.
Every reaction narrows paths.
Every visible move commits you further.

Sun Tzu warns against forcing outcomes prematurely:

> "Do not press a desperate foe too hard."

Why? Because desperation collapses optionality for *both* sides. It forces terminal outcomes where maneuver once existed.

AWH principle:

> **Restraint delays irreversibility.**

And delaying irreversibility is one of the highest forms of strategic intelligence.

Restraint and Timing Discipline

Restraint is inseparable from timing.

Early action destroys timing.
Late action forces timing.
Restraint *protects* timing.

Sun Tzu's emphasis on "when" rather than "how" reflects this:

> "He will win who knows when to fight and when not to fight."

Restraint is what allows you to wait for the moment when action becomes cheap, safe, and decisive.

AWH language:

> **Restraint keeps you available for the correct moment.**

Without restraint, you arrive exhausted—or too early—or too late.

Restraint and Information Maturity

Information is always incomplete. Acting on immature information amplifies error.

Restraint allows:

- Weak signals to clarify
- Noise to dissipate
- Opponent intentions to surface

Sun Tzu's reliance on intelligence is not about collecting more data—it is about allowing meaning to emerge.

> "Spies are a most important element in war."

Intelligence requires time. Interpretation requires patience. Restraint provides both.

AWH reframes this as **interpretive patience**: allowing understanding to mature before commitment.

Restraint and Cost Containment

Restraint is one of the most effective cost-control mechanisms available.

Unrestrained systems spend continuously:

- Responding
- Defending
- Explaining
- Correcting

Restrained systems spend selectively.

Sun Tzu repeatedly emphasizes economy of force:

> "The clever combatant looks to the effect of combined energy."

Combined energy is conserved energy. Restraint prevents dissipation.

AWH language is explicit:

What you do not do cannot cost you.

This is not minimalism. It is efficiency.

Restraint Versus Suppression

Restraint is not suppression.

Suppression avoids action because of fear or incapacity. Restraint avoids action because action is unnecessary or counterproductive.

The difference is structural.

Suppression leaks:

- Frustration
- Resentment
- Unresolved tension

Restraint accumulates:

- Leverage
- Readiness
- Advantage

Sun Tzu praises the latter and avoids the former.

Restraint and Visibility Control

Restraint limits visibility.

Every action reveals intent.
Every response signals priority.
Every escalation attracts attention.

Sun Tzu's preference for obscurity reflects this:

> "The general who is skilled in defense hides in the
> most secret recesses of the earth."

Restraint keeps you unreadable. It denies others the information
they need to adapt against you.

AWH language:

> **Restraint preserves ambiguity. Ambiguity
> preserves power.**

Restraint in Leadership

Leaders are often pressured to intervene.

Teams expect answers.
Stakeholders expect response.
Observers expect decisiveness.

Sun Tzu resists this pressure entirely.

> "If words of command are not clear and distinct, if orders are not thoroughly understood, the general is to blame."

Clear orders are rare. Unnecessary orders are destructive.

Restraint in leadership looks like:

- Fewer directives
- Clearer thresholds
- Less micromanagement
- More structural alignment

AWH principle:

> **Intervention should be rare enough to matter when it occurs.**

Restraint and Ego Discipline

Ego is the greatest enemy of restraint.

Ego demands response.
Ego demands recognition.
Ego demands visible assertion.

Sun Tzu identifies ego-driven failure repeatedly:

"The general who is choleric and quick-tempered may be provoked by insults."

Insults only work when ego overrides discipline.

AWH language is unforgiving:

Ego converts restraint into perceived weakness—and action into self-harm.

True restraint requires emotional control, not intellectual sophistication.

Restraint and Long-Term Advantage

Short-term action often produces long-term disadvantage.

Restraint in the short term often creates:

- Strategic exhaustion in others
- Unforced errors by opponents
- Natural resolution of conflict
- Cheaper opportunities later

Sun Tzu relies on this dynamic constantly.

"If the enemy is taking his ease, give him no rest."

Note: *not* "attack him." Pressure does not require action. Often it requires *withholding* it.

AWH reframes this as **pressure through patience**.

When Restraint Fails

Restraint fails when it becomes:

- Avoidance
- Fear-based paralysis
- Excuse for inaction

Sun Tzu does not advocate endless waiting. He advocates *disciplined waiting*.

There is a point where restraint becomes decay—when costs compound, posture weakens, or opportunity closes.

AWH language is clear:

> **Restraint must improve position.**
> **If it does not, it is no longer restraint.**

When Action Becomes Necessary

Restraint is not permanent.

Action becomes necessary when:

- Delay increases cost

- Risk begins to compound
- Optionality collapses
- Timing shifts against you

Sun Tzu recognizes this balance:

"Let your rapidity be that of the wind."

Speed is required *after* restraint has done its work.

AWH principle:

Restraint prepares the ground so that action, when taken, is decisive.

Restraint as Ethical Responsibility

There is an ethical dimension to restraint that Sun Tzu never sentimentalizes, but clearly understands.

Unnecessary action shifts cost onto others:

- Soldiers
- Workers
- Families
- Institutions

Restraint is how leaders honor responsibility.

"The general is the bulwark of the State."

A bulwark absorbs pressure. It does not transmit it unnecessarily.

AWH language is explicit:

> **Those who command owe restraint to those who bear consequence.**

Restraint and the Illusion of Control

Action creates the illusion of control. Restraint reveals its limits.

Sun Tzu does not promise control. He promises **position**.

Position allows influence without constant action.

AWH reframes this:

> **Control is fragile. Position is durable.**

Restraint builds position.

The Core Art of War Truth Restated

> **The best action is often the one not taken.**

Not because action is bad.
Not because conflict is avoidable.
But because unnecessary action creates unnecessary cost.

Sun Tzu's system is not aggressive. It is **selective**.

It acts only when:

- Cost is acceptable
- Risk is bounded
- Timing is correct
- Preparation is complete
- Visibility is controlled

Everything else is restraint.

Closing Orientation

This chapter establishes **Restraint** as a decision primitive because it is the discipline that binds all others together.

Restraint:

- Preserves resources
- Prevents escalation
- Protects optionality
- Enables timing
- Makes preparation matter

Without restraint, cost accelerates.
Without restraint, risk compounds.
Without restraint, visibility becomes exposure.

Sun Tzu did not win by doing more.
He won by **doing less—at the right times, for the right reasons**.

Ancient Wisdom Hacks makes this explicit:

> **Strength is not measured by how often you act.**
> **It is measured by how often you do not need to.**

That is not weakness.

That is mastery.

PART III

THE ORDER OF DECISION

(Why sequence matters more than intelligence)

Chapter 11

Why Decisions Must Be Ordered

Introduction: Intelligence Fails Without Sequence

Most strategic failures are misdiagnosed.

They are blamed on poor intelligence.
They are blamed on bad luck.
They are blamed on weak execution.

In reality, many failures occur **despite** good intelligence, favorable conditions, and competent execution.

They occur because the **order of decision was wrong**.

Correct actions taken in the wrong sequence produce failure that looks inexplicable after the fact. Teams say, *"We did everything right."* They did—but not in the right order.

The Art of War is not a book of clever ideas. It is a book of sequence. It assumes that outcomes are determined less by what you do than *when* and *in what order* you do it.

This chapter formalizes a principle that modern strategy consistently ignores:

> **Sequence governs outcome more reliably than intelligence.**

A decision system without order is not a system. It is a collection of impulses dressed up as analysis.

The Hidden Failure Pattern: Right Move, Wrong Time

Consider the most common post-mortem explanation in failed initiatives:

- "The idea was sound."
- "The data supported it."
- "The team executed well."

And yet—collapse.

This paradox only exists if you assume decisions are independent events. They are not.

Decisions are **cascades**. Each step constrains the next. Each action alters cost, risk, information, timing, visibility, and optionality.

Sun Tzu understood this implicitly. He never presents principles as interchangeable. He presents them as **ordered constraints**.

> "The general who wins a battle makes many calculations in his temple before the battle is fought."

Calculations precede movement. Assessment precedes commitment. Position precedes engagement.

AWH language is precise here:

Sequence is the architecture of decision-making.

Without it, intelligence becomes a liability.

Why Sequence Matters More Than Intelligence

Intelligence answers *what is true.*
Sequence determines *what becomes possible.*

You can know everything and still fail if you act out of order.

Examples are everywhere:

- Accurate data acted on before cost is understood
- Correct strategy executed before timing is favorable
- Strong preparation followed by premature visibility
- Valid risk assessment ignored because action felt urgent

Sun Tzu never argues that knowledge alone wins wars. He argues that **knowledge applied in the wrong order loses them**.

> "If you know the enemy and know yourself, you need not fear the result of a hundred battles."

This statement is conditional. "Know" does not mean "possess facts." It means *apply understanding correctly*—which includes sequence.

AWH reframes this bluntly:

Intelligence without order accelerates error.

Most Failures Come From Correct Actions Taken in the Wrong Sequence

This is the central claim of Part III.

Failure does not usually come from doing the wrong thing.
It comes from doing the right thing **too early, too late, or before prerequisites are satisfied**.

Examples:

- Acting before cost is bounded
- Scaling before systems stabilize
- Negotiating before leverage exists
- Revealing intent before position is secure

Sun Tzu warns against this repeatedly, though never explicitly naming "sequence":

> "Move not unless you see an advantage; use not your troops unless there is something to be gained."

Advantage must precede movement. Gain must precede commitment. These are ordering rules.

AWH language clarifies the pattern:

Premature correctness is indistinguishable from error.

Skipping Steps Creates False Confidence

One of the most dangerous side effects of sequence violation is **false confidence**.

When steps are skipped:

- Early wins appear to validate bad structure
- Momentum masks exposure
- Confidence rises faster than resilience

Sun Tzu warns against this through his emphasis on discipline over heroics:

> "In war, discipline is more important than numbers."

Numbers—like early results—can deceive. Discipline enforces order even when confidence tempts shortcuts.

False confidence is particularly dangerous because it feels earned. It is reinforced by partial success and social validation.

AWH language is explicit:

> **Confidence gained by skipping steps is borrowed time.**

It collapses the moment conditions shift.

Action Without Order Magnifies Error

Action is an amplifier.

If structure is sound, action multiplies advantage.
If structure is flawed, action multiplies damage.

Sun Tzu understands this asymmetry:

> "The general who loses a battle makes but few calculations beforehand."

The error is not action itself. It is action taken **before calculation is complete**.

AWH reframes this as a rule:

Action should be the last step, not the first response.

When action is taken out of order, it converts small errors into irreversible losses.

The Art of War Is a Sequence Manual

Despite modern interpretations, *The Art of War* is not a list of tips. It is a **procedural system**.

Look at its internal logic:

1. Define the stakes (life or death, survival or ruin)
2. Assess fundamental conditions (the five constant factors)
3. Evaluate cost and logistics
4. Secure intelligence and deception
5. Shape timing and position
6. Engage only when advantage is assured

This is an order.

Sun Tzu does not allow reordering. He does not suggest improvising the sequence. He insists on it—implicitly, relentlessly.

AWH language names what Sun Tzu assumed:

Sequence is non-negotiable because reality is unforgiving.

Why Modern Strategy Breaks Sequence

Modern decision environments actively encourage sequence violations.

They reward:

- Speed over structure
- Visibility over preparation
- Action over restraint

This creates systemic pressure to:

- Announce before preparing
- Act before understanding
- Commit before optionality is preserved

Sun Tzu's system is incompatible with these incentives. That is precisely why it remains relevant.

> "He who exercises no forethought but makes light of his opponents is sure to be captured by them."

Forethought is sequence discipline.

AWH language is blunt:

Culture rewards motion. Reality rewards order.

Sequence and the Illusion of Agility

Agility is often used to justify skipping steps.

"We'll adjust as we go."
"We can pivot."
"We'll fix it later."

Sun Tzu would reject this logic entirely.

Adjustment is only possible when:

- Costs are contained
- Risk is bounded
- Visibility is controlled
- Optionality remains

Those conditions are created by *following sequence*, not ignoring it.

AWH reframes agility correctly:

True agility comes from ordered preparation, not reactive improvisation.

The Compounding Effect of Early Errors

Sequence violations compound.

An early error:

- Forces compensatory actions
- Increases visibility
- Accelerates cost
- Narrows options

Each compensatory step adds complexity and fragility.

Sun Tzu avoids this trap by refusing to act until prerequisites are satisfied.

> "Victorious warriors win first and then go to war, while defeated warriors go to war first and then seek to win."

Seeking to win *after* engagement is already a sequence failure.

Order as Risk Management

Sequence is the primary mechanism for risk reduction.

By ordering decisions correctly, you:

- Identify exposure before commitment
- Reduce irreversible moves
- Delay escalation
- Preserve exits

Sun Tzu's emphasis on calculation before battle is risk discipline, not caution.

AWH language:

Order transforms uncertainty into survivable risk.

Why Intelligence Is Overrated

Intelligence is seductive.

It feels sophisticated.
It feels empowering.
It feels sufficient.

But intelligence does not enforce order.

Highly intelligent teams often fail faster because they are more confident skipping steps. They believe insight compensates for structure.

Sun Tzu does not confuse insight with discipline.

> "The wise sovereign and the good general are able to strike and conquer… because they know what is essential."

Knowing what is essential includes knowing *what must come first*.

AWH reframes this as:

Order disciplines intelligence so it does not become reckless.

The Decision Stack: AWH Ordering Logic

Within the AWH framework, decisions must follow a fixed order:

1. **Constraint** – What cannot be changed
2. **Cost** – What will be consumed
3. **Risk** – What exposure exists
4. **Information** – What is known and unknown
5. **Timing** – When action is permissible
6. **Preparation** – Whether uncertainty is bounded
7. **Visibility** – What will be revealed
8. **Restraint** – What should not be done
9. **Action** – Only now

Skipping any step invalidates the ones that follow.

Sun Tzu never lists this stack explicitly—but he never violates it either.

Sequence and Authority

Order is a leadership responsibility.

Execution can be delegated.
Analysis can be delegated.
Sequence cannot.

When leaders allow teams to act out of order, they are not empowering them—they are **abdicating structure**.

Sun Tzu assigns this responsibility clearly:

> "The general is the bulwark of the State."

A bulwark holds sequence under pressure.

AWH language is clear:

> **Authority exists to enforce order when urgency tempts shortcuts.**

Why Sequence Feels Slow—and Why That's Deceptive

Correct sequence often feels slow at the beginning.

There is analysis.
There is waiting.
There is restraint.

But once action begins, execution is fast, clean, and decisive—because friction has already been removed.

Sun Tzu captures this paradox:

> "Let your rapidity be that of the wind."

Rapidity comes *after* order.

AWH reframes the paradox:

> **Sequence front-loads slowness to enable speed later.**

The Psychological Cost of Order

Order is psychologically demanding.

It requires:

- Saying no to premature action
- Tolerating ambiguity
- Resisting pressure
- Withstanding criticism

Sun Tzu's unemotional tone reflects the emotional discipline required.

AWH language is blunt:

> **Most people do not fail because they lack intelligence.**
> **They fail because they cannot tolerate sequence.**

The Illusion of Progress

Out-of-order action creates the illusion of progress.

Meetings happen.
Announcements are made.
Resources move.

But structure deteriorates.

Sun Tzu avoids this by valuing outcomes over activity.

> "In war, then, let your great object be victory, not
> lengthy campaigns."

Lengthy campaigns are often the result of sequence failure.

Order Prevents Escalation

Escalation often begins when action precedes preparation or
restraint.

Sequence prevents escalation by:

- Forcing cost assessment first
- Enforcing visibility control
- Delaying commitment

Sun Tzu's preference for avoidance reflects this discipline.

AWH language:

Order is how you win without fighting.

Why Sequence Cannot Be Fixed Later

Once action begins out of order, sequence cannot be repaired cheaply.

Costs are sunk.
Visibility is triggered.
Options collapse.

Sun Tzu never proposes mid-battle reordering. He proposes avoiding the battle entirely until order is complete.

The Central Warning of This Chapter

This chapter exists to dismantle a comforting myth:

> *If we are smart enough, we can fix mistakes as we go.*

Sun Tzu knew better.

AWH states it plainly:

> **Correct actions taken in the wrong order are still mistakes.**

Closing Orientation

This chapter establishes why **order is the spine of strategy**.

Not intelligence.
Not courage.
Not speed.

Order.

Without order:

- Intelligence accelerates error
- Action magnifies damage
- Confidence becomes fragility

With order:

- Small advantages compound
- Risk is contained
- Action becomes decisive

Sun Tzu did not outthink his opponents by being clever.

He outlasted and outmaneuvered them by **never violating sequence**.

Ancient Wisdom Hacks makes this explicit:

> **Strategy does not fail because people choose the wrong actions.**
> **It fails because they choose them in the wrong order.**

Everything that follows in this framework depends on respecting that truth.

Chapter 12

The Decision Sequence (Canonical)

Introduction: Why a Canonical Sequence Must Exist

Strategy fails most often not because people misunderstand principles, but because they **apply them out of order**.

They assess risk before cost.
They act before preparation.
They reveal before positioning.
They move before restraint has done its work.

Each of these errors is survivable in isolation. Together, they are fatal.

The Art of War is frequently read as a book of insights. It is not. It is a book of *order*. Its principles are not interchangeable. They form a sequence that mirrors reality itself.

This chapter formalizes that sequence.

Not as a suggestion.
Not as a heuristic.
But as a **canonical decision order**—a fixed progression that must be followed if decisions are to remain survivable under pressure.

This sequence is non-negotiable.

Not because of tradition.
Not because of doctrine.
But because violating it consistently produces the same failures,
across centuries, domains, and technologies.

Why a Canonical Order Is Necessary

Modern decision-making frameworks often pride themselves on
flexibility. They encourage iteration, parallel analysis, and adaptive
loops.

This works only in environments where:

- Errors are cheap
- Reversibility is high
- Visibility is low
- Time is forgiving

Strategic reality rarely offers these conditions.

Sun Tzu assumes the opposite:

- Errors compound
- Commitments harden quickly
- Visibility triggers reaction
- Time punishes weakness

Under these conditions, **order becomes protection**.

AWH language is precise:

> **Sequence is how strategy survives contact with reality.**

Without a fixed order, decision-makers substitute intuition, urgency, or ego for structure. The result is motion without control.

The Canonical Decision Sequence (Overview)

The AWH framework mandates the following sequence—always, without exception:

1. **Assess Constraint**
2. **Identify Cost**
3. **Bound Risk**
4. **Evaluate Timing**
5. **Prepare Position**
6. **Control Visibility**
7. **Apply Restraint**
8. **Act Only If Action Reduces Total Cost**

Each step gates the next.
Each step eliminates failure modes introduced by premature progression.

Skipping a step does not save time. It **transfers cost forward**, where it multiplies.

Sun Tzu never violates this order. Neither can you—if survivability matters.

Step 1: Assess Constraint

All strategy begins inside constraint.

Constraint is not a limitation to overcome; it is the **boundary of reality**.

Constraint includes:

- Immutable facts
- Non-negotiable limits
- Structural asymmetries
- External forces beyond influence

Sun Tzu opens his work by defining the domain:

> "War is a matter of vital importance to the State; the province of life or death; the road to survival or ruin."

This is constraint framing. Before tactics, before ambition, before movement, the limits are established.

AWH rule:

> **If you have not named the constraints, you are fantasizing, not strategizing.**

Why this step must come first:

- Constraints cannot be optimized away
- Ignored constraints reassert themselves later as catastrophe
- All subsequent analysis depends on what cannot change

Any attempt to identify cost, risk, or timing before constraints are explicit is structurally invalid.

Step 2: Identify Cost

Once constraints are known, cost becomes legible.

Cost is not what you pay later.
Cost is what you are already exposed to.

This includes:

- Direct costs
- Indirect costs
- Compounding costs
- Opportunity costs
- Optionality loss

Sun Tzu repeatedly emphasizes burden before action:

> "There is no instance of a nation benefiting from prolonged warfare."

Why? Because cost accumulates long before outcomes are visible.

AWH discipline:

Cost must be identified before it is justified.

Why this step must follow constraint:

- Cost is meaningless without boundaries
- Some costs are unacceptable regardless of upside
- You cannot evaluate risk until you know what loss matters

Skipping this step leads to a classic failure mode: *winning that destroys the future.*

Step 3: Bound Risk

Risk is not probability.
Risk is **exposure to loss**.

Once cost is identified, risk can be bounded.

Bounding risk means:

- Identifying worst-case outcomes
- Assessing irreversibility
- Ensuring survivability if failure occurs

Sun Tzu never asks how likely defeat is. He asks whether defeat can be tolerated.

> "If you know the enemy and know yourself, you need
> not fear the result of a hundred battles."

This is exposure control, not prediction.

AWH rule:

If risk cannot be bounded, action is prohibited.

Why this step must follow cost:

- Risk cannot be evaluated without knowing what is at stake
- Some risks are unacceptable regardless of likelihood
- Probability-based thinking fails in asymmetric, irreversible domains

Risk unmanaged does not disappear. It becomes cost realized.

Step 4: Evaluate Timing

Only after constraint, cost, and risk are understood does timing become meaningful.

Timing answers:

- Does time favor us or others?
- Will delay reduce or increase cost?
- Will action now reduce exposure—or amplify it?

Sun Tzu is explicit:

> "He will win who knows when to fight and when not to fight."

Timing is not urgency. It is **structural permission**.

AWH discipline:

If timing is unclear, action is premature.

Why this step must follow risk:

- Acting too early exposes bounded risk to unnecessary amplification
- Acting too late converts manageable risk into forced loss
- Timing determines whether action reduces or multiplies exposure

Without this step, speed masquerades as decisiveness.

Step 5: Prepare Position

Preparation is where uncertainty is converted into bounded risk.

Preparation includes:

- Resource staging
- Information filtering
- Scenario mapping
- Authority alignment
- Exit definition

Sun Tzu states this without ambiguity:

"Victorious warriors win first and then go to war."

Winning first is preparation.

AWH rule:

If preparation is incomplete, timing is an illusion.

Why this step must follow timing:

- Preparation without timing leads to decay
- Timing without preparation leads to exposure
- The two only function together

Prepared positions exert leverage without movement.

Step 6: Control Visibility

Only after position is prepared does visibility become a consideration.

Visibility is not neutral. It triggers:

- Attention
- Resistance
- Counteraction

Sun Tzu's preference for obscurity is consistent:

> "When able to attack, we must seem unable; when using our forces, we must seem inactive."

AWH principle:

Visibility is a liability unless deliberately traded.

Why this step must follow preparation:

- Visibility before preparation invites preemption
- Visibility without position collapses optionality
- Prepared visibility can be weaponized; unprepared visibility cannot

Many failures occur here—through premature announcements, signaling, or public commitment.

Step 7: Apply Restraint

Restraint is the active decision **not** to act yet.

It preserves:

- Resources
- Timing
- Optionality
- Emotional discipline

Sun Tzu frames restraint as mastery:

> "He who knows when he can fight and when he cannot, will be victorious."

AWH discipline:

Restraint is the final filter before action.

Why this step must precede action:

- It prevents ego-driven escalation
- It allows last signals to surface
- It ensures action is necessary, not merely possible

Restraint is how strategy resists pressure to move prematurely.

Step 8: Act Only If Action Reduces Total Cost

This is the final gate.

Action is permitted **only if** it reduces total cost across time, not merely produces short-term gain.

This includes:

- Reduced exposure
- Faster resolution
- Preserved optionality
- Lower long-term burden

Sun Tzu defines success this way:

> "To subdue the enemy without fighting is the acme of skill."

Action is not the goal. *Cost reduction is.*

AWH rule, stated plainly:

If action does not reduce total cost, it is not strategic.

Why This Sequence Is Non-Negotiable

Each step exists to prevent a specific failure mode:

- Constraint prevents fantasy
- Cost prevents hollow victory
- Risk prevents catastrophe
- Timing prevents premature exposure
- Preparation prevents chaos
- Visibility prevents reaction traps
- Restraint prevents escalation
- Action, when finally taken, resolves rather than compounds

Reordering these steps does not create flexibility. It creates fragility.

Sun Tzu never rearranges this logic. Neither should you.

Common Violations and Their Consequences

Action before preparation → irreversible exposure
Visibility before position → accelerated opposition
Risk after commitment → forced loss
Timing ignored → urgency-driven failure

These are not theoretical. They are the repeating patterns of strategic collapse.

Why Leaders Resist This Sequence

Because it demands:

- Patience
- Emotional control
- Saying no to momentum
- Withstanding criticism

Sun Tzu's unemotional tone reflects the discipline required.

AWH language is blunt:

> **Most people do not fail because they lack intelligence.**
> **They fail because they cannot tolerate order.**

The Sequence as a Strategic Spine

This chapter completes Part III by making explicit what *The Art of War* assumes throughout:

Order is the spine of strategy.

Not ideas.
Not brilliance.
Not speed.

Order.

Closing Orientation

This chapter does not ask you to agree with the canonical sequence.

It warns you what happens if you violate it.

Sun Tzu did not win by improvising.
He won by **never acting before reality allowed him to**.

Ancient Wisdom Hacks makes that discipline explicit:

**You do not earn the right to act by wanting to.
You earn it by surviving every step that comes before.**

This sequence is non-negotiable.

Everything that follows depends on it.

Chapter 13

When Not to Decide

Introduction: The Most Dangerous Assumption in Strategy

Modern strategy culture treats indecision as failure.

If you do not decide, you are weak.
If you wait, you are losing ground.
If you hesitate, someone else will move first.

This belief is deeply ingrained—and profoundly destructive.

The Art of War does not share this assumption. Sun Tzu does not assume that decisions must always be made immediately. He assumes the opposite: that **many decisions become worse the moment they are forced**, and better when they are withheld.

This chapter formalizes a discipline that is rarely taught and often punished:

> **Knowing when *not* to decide is as important as knowing what to decide.**

Not all delays are avoidance.
Not all non-decisions are weakness.
And not all choices deserve to be made yet.

Decision Avoidance vs. Strategic Delay

The first distinction must be absolute and uncompromising.

Decision Avoidance

Decision avoidance is passive, fear-driven, and corrosive.

It looks like:

- Postponement without preparation
- Silence without positioning
- Waiting because of anxiety or indecision
- Hoping problems disappear

Avoidance leaks confidence. It increases internal tension. It allows cost and risk to accumulate unchecked.

Sun Tzu never advocates avoidance.

Strategic Delay

Strategic delay is active, intentional, and disciplined.

It looks like:

- Waiting while posture improves
- Holding while information clarifies
- Restraining action to preserve optionality
- Allowing others to incur cost

Sun Tzu advocates this constantly.

> "He who is prudent and lies in wait for an enemy who is not, will be victorious."

This is not indecision. It is **deliberate non-commitment**.

AWH language draws the line clearly:

Avoidance is waiting because you cannot act. Strategic delay is waiting because you do not need to.

Why the Urge to Decide Is So Strong

Decisions provide psychological relief.

They resolve tension.
They signal control.
They quiet anxiety.

Non-decisions do the opposite. They prolong uncertainty and invite judgment.

This creates a powerful bias toward premature choice.

Sun Tzu understood this weakness and designed his system to neutralize it. His writing removes emotion from the equation. He does not ask what *feels* right. He asks what *reduces exposure*.

"The general who is choleric and quick-tempered may
be provoked by insults."

Provocation is a forcing mechanism. It exists to **extract a
decision before conditions are favorable**.

AWH language is blunt:

> **Most bad decisions are made to relieve emotional
> pressure, not strategic necessity.**

Waiting as an Active Posture

Waiting is not inactivity.

Waiting is posture.

An active waiting posture includes:

- Resource conservation
- Information monitoring
- Opponent observation
- Option preservation
- Preparation without commitment

Sun Tzu frames this repeatedly as "lying in wait," "remaining at
ease," or "holding position."

> "He who occupies the field of battle first and awaits
> his enemy is at ease."

Being "at ease" is not laziness. It is **structural advantage**.

AWH reframes waiting as **strategic stillness**—a state in which you are ready to act, but not required to.

Letting Conditions Resolve Themselves

One of the most counterintuitive truths in strategy is this:

> Many problems do not need to be solved.
> They need to be *outlasted*.

Time is not neutral. It erodes weak positions, exposes fragile strategies, and exhausts overextended actors.

Sun Tzu relies on this dynamic constantly.

He does not rush to confront strength. He waits for imbalance.

> "If the enemy is taking his ease, give him no rest. If
> his forces are united, separate them."

Note: this is not always done through direct action. Often it is done by **withholding action**, allowing internal contradictions to surface.

AWH principle:

Time is an ally when others are mispositioned.

Letting conditions resolve themselves is not abdication. It is **cost displacement**—allowing time to work against others instead of against you.

Why Some Decisions Improve by Not Being Made

This chapter introduces a rule that feels heretical in modern decision culture:

Some decisions improve by not being made.

This happens when delay:

- Reveals hidden costs
- Clarifies information
- Shifts leverage
- Forces others to act first
- Collapses false urgency

Sun Tzu never treats first-move advantage as inherently superior. He often treats it as a liability.

"When able to attack, we must seem unable."

Why? Because premature clarity invites adaptation.

AWH language is precise:

**Decisions made under incomplete conditions
often lock in the worst possible version of reality.**

Waiting allows reality to finish forming.

The Decision That Forces Commitment

Some decisions are irreversible.

Once made, they:

- Trigger visibility
- Collapse optionality
- Accelerate escalation
- Convert risk into cost

These decisions demand restraint.

Sun Tzu repeatedly warns against premature commitment:

> "There are roads which must not be followed, armies
> which must not be attacked, towns which must not be
> besieged."

These are not absolute prohibitions. They are *timing prohibitions*.

AWH reframes this clearly:

**If a decision forces commitment before advantage
is secured, it should not be made yet.**

Decision Pressure as a Strategic Signal

Pressure to decide is itself information.

When others push for resolution:

- They may benefit from your commitment
- They may be hiding weakness
- They may need clarity more than you do

Sun Tzu exploits this asymmetry constantly.

> "If the enemy leaves a door open, you must rush in."

But note: *you* choose when to rush in. You do not rush simply because a door exists.

AWH language:

> **Pressure to decide often indicates that waiting is advantageous.**

The Trap of "Decide or Die"

Modern leadership culture frames indecision as existential risk.

In reality, **premature decisions create the very danger they claim to avoid.**

Sun Tzu's system is built to survive prolonged ambiguity.

> "In war, discipline is more important than numbers."

Discipline includes the discipline to *not decide* until structure is ready.

AWH principle:

> **Decide late, not early—unless delay increases cost.**

When Waiting Becomes Dangerous

This chapter does not romanticize delay.

Waiting becomes dangerous when:

- Costs compound silently
- Risk escalates asymmetrically
- Tolerance erodes
- Timing shifts against you

Sun Tzu condemns prolonged warfare not because it involves waiting, but because it involves **waiting without positional improvement**.

> "There is no instance of a nation benefiting from prolonged warfare."

AWH language clarifies the boundary:

**Waiting must improve position.
If it does not, it is decay—not strategy.**

Decision Readiness vs. Decision Urgency

Urgency is emotional.
Readiness is structural.

Many decisions feel urgent long before they are ready.

Sun Tzu refuses to act on urgency alone.

> "Move not unless you see an advantage."

Advantage is readiness, not pressure.

AWH reframes the distinction:

> **A decision is ready when not deciding becomes
> more expensive than deciding.**

Until that point, restraint dominates.

The Cost of Premature Resolution

Resolution feels satisfying. It closes loops. It creates narrative clarity.

But premature resolution:

- Locks in assumptions
- Freezes flexibility
- Prevents learning
- Transfers leverage outward

Sun Tzu avoids resolution until outcome is constrained.

> "Victorious warriors win first and then go to war."

Winning first means *deciding late*—after structure has already determined the result.

Letting Others Decide First

One of the most powerful uses of strategic delay is **forcing others to decide first**.

When they do:

- They reveal intent
- They incur visibility
- They commit resources
- They narrow options

Sun Tzu legitimizes this posture:

> "If the enemy is in superior strength, evade him."

Evasion is not retreat. It is **decision displacement**.

AWH language:

> **Let others spend commitment while you retain freedom.**

The Emotional Discipline of Not Deciding

Not deciding requires emotional control.

It invites:

- Criticism
- Second-guessing
- Pressure from stakeholders
- Accusations of weakness

Sun Tzu's unemotional tone reflects this requirement.

AWH language is blunt:

> **Most people decide too early because they cannot tolerate being judged while waiting.**

Strategic leaders accept this discomfort.

The Canonical Test: Should This Decision Be Made Now?

Before deciding, the framework demands these questions:

1. Does deciding now reduce total cost?
2. Does delay improve or worsen posture?
3. Will information meaningfully clarify with time?
4. Does this decision force irreversible commitment?
5. Who benefits more from resolution—us or others?

If answers favor delay, **not deciding is the correct move**.

When Not Deciding *Is* the Decision

Non-decision is not neutral.

Choosing not to decide is itself a decision—to preserve optionality, to displace cost, to wait for structure.

Sun Tzu's entire system relies on this implicit choice.

> "He who knows when he can fight and when he cannot will be victorious."

Knowing when you *cannot* fight is knowing when not to decide.

Counterintuitive Rule Restated

Some decisions improve by not being made.

Not forever.
Not blindly.
But until structure replaces urgency.

This rule feels wrong to action-oriented cultures. It feels dangerous. It feels irresponsible.

It is none of those things.

It is **disciplined patience**.

Closing Orientation

This chapter completes the logic of Part III by addressing the final, most difficult discipline: restraint at the level of decision itself.

Sun Tzu did not rush to decide.
He waited until decisions became unavoidable for others—and optional for him.

Ancient Wisdom Hacks makes the discipline explicit:

> **You are not obligated to decide simply because a choice exists.**
> **You are obligated to decide only when not deciding becomes more dangerous than acting.**

That is not indecision.

That is mastery of sequence, cost, risk, timing, and restraint.

And it is one of the rarest strategic skills in any era.

PART IV

FAILURE MODES

(How the system breaks when misused)

Chapter 14

Emotional Contamination

Introduction: When the System Is Intact—but the Operator Is Not

Most strategic failures are not caused by ignorance.

They are caused by **contamination**.

The framework may be correct.
The sequence may be understood.
The primitives may be known.

And still—collapse.

Why?

Because strategy is executed by humans, and humans are vulnerable to emotional interference. When emotion enters the decision process unchecked, it does not merely influence outcomes—it **reorders the system**, bypasses constraints, and justifies violations that would otherwise be rejected immediately.

The Art of War is often mischaracterized as cold or ruthless. In truth, it is psychologically precise. Sun Tzu understands that the greatest threat to strategic clarity is not the enemy—it is the commander's own emotional state.

This chapter examines the most common and most destructive failure mode in the entire framework:

> **Emotional contamination—when pride, fear, urgency, or ego distort judgment and override order.**

Emotional Contamination Defined

Emotional contamination occurs when affective states:

- Bypass sequence
- Distort cost perception
- Collapse risk discipline
- Force premature action

It does not look irrational in the moment. On the contrary, emotional decisions often feel **clear, strong, and decisive**. That is what makes them dangerous.

AWH language is direct:

> **Emotional contamination does not announce itself as error.**
> **It announces itself as certainty.**

Why Emotion Is So Dangerous in Strategy

Emotion is not inherently bad.

Emotion provides motivation, cohesion, and resilience. But **emotion is a poor ordering mechanism**. It prioritizes relief over accuracy and resolution over survivability.

Sun Tzu understood this deeply. His work contains repeated warnings—not about tactics, but about temperament.

> "The general who is choleric and quick-tempered may be provoked by insults."

This is not a character critique. It is a systems warning.

Provocation exists to **trigger emotional reordering**—to make you act before constraint, cost, risk, and timing have been respected.

Pride: The Most Expensive Emotion

How Pride Enters the System

Pride manifests as:

- Attachment to reputation
- Refusal to disengage
- Escalation to "save face"
- Resistance to reversal

Pride transforms optional situations into existential ones.

Sun Tzu names this explicitly:

> "If the general regards his soldiers as his children, but is unable to employ them strictly, the army will be disorganized."

This reflects a deeper truth: **ego-driven leadership confuses identity with outcome**.

AWH language is blunt:

> **Pride converts reversible loss into irreversible commitment.**

Pride and Escalation Traps

Pride prevents:

- Retreat
- Delay
- Non-decision
- Admission of error

It reframes restraint as humiliation and escalation as honor.

Sun Tzu rejects this framing entirely. His system has no concept of honor-based action. There is only cost and survival.

> "The supreme art of war is to subdue the enemy without fighting."

Fighting to preserve pride is not strategy. It is emotional indulgence paid for with real resources.

Fear: The Accelerator of Bad Decisions

How Fear Distorts Judgment

Fear compresses time.

It creates urgency where none exists.
It magnifies downside while obscuring structure.
It demands immediate action to relieve discomfort.

Fear-driven decisions feel responsible. They often masquerade as "risk management."

Sun Tzu warns against this indirectly through his insistence on preparation and restraint.

> "If you know yourself but not the enemy, for every victory gained you will also suffer a defeat."

Fear narrows perception. It substitutes imagined threats for assessed ones.

AWH principle:

**Fear does not reduce risk.
It accelerates exposure.**

Fear and Premature Action

Fear leads to:

- Overreaction to weak signals
- Defensive escalation
- Visibility before preparation
- Action without timing

These actions feel protective. They are not.

Sun Tzu's system treats fear as noise, not input.

AWH language clarifies:

If a decision is being made to relieve fear, it is already compromised.

Urgency: The Most Convincing Lie

Urgency is the most socially acceptable form of emotional contamination.

It is praised.
It is rewarded.
It is rarely questioned.

Urgency reframes emotional pressure as structural necessity.

Sun Tzu explicitly rejects urgency-driven action:

> "Move not unless you see an advantage."

Advantage is not urgency. Urgency is an internal sensation. Advantage is an external condition.

AWH rule:

Urgency is not evidence.

How Urgency Breaks Sequence

Urgency causes:

- Cost to be justified after action
- Risk to be accepted implicitly
- Timing to be ignored

- Preparation to be abbreviated

Each violation compounds the next.

Sun Tzu's emphasis on calculation before battle is designed to neutralize urgency.

> "The general who wins a battle makes many calculations in his temple before the battle is fought."

Calculations do not coexist with urgency. One must dominate the other.

Ego: The Silent System Corruptor

Ego is not arrogance alone.

Ego includes:

- Overconfidence
- Identity attachment
- Narrative preservation
- Need for recognition

Ego contaminates judgment by **shifting the decision's objective**—from outcome optimization to self-validation.

Sun Tzu addresses ego repeatedly, though indirectly:

> "If a general shows confidence in his men but always insists on his orders being obeyed, the gain will be mutual."

Confidence without rigidity. Authority without ego.

AWH language is unforgiving:

Ego turns strategy into performance.

Performance is costly. Strategy is efficient.

Emotional Decisions Feel Decisive—but Cost More

One of the most dangerous properties of emotional decisions is how they feel.

They feel:

- Clean
- Resolute
- Powerful
- Final

This sensation is addictive.

But decisiveness is not effectiveness.

Sun Tzu never praises decisiveness for its own sake. He praises **outcomes achieved with minimal expenditure**.

> "In war, then, let your great object be victory, not lengthy campaigns."

Lengthy campaigns are often driven by emotional escalation—by decisions made to feel decisive rather than to reduce cost.

AWH principle:

> **If a decision feels emotionally satisfying, scrutinize it twice.**

Confidence Is Not Clarity

Confidence is internal.
Clarity is structural.

They are not correlated.

Emotionally contaminated decisions often come with *high confidence* and *low clarity*.

Sun Tzu distinguishes clearly between the two:

> "The wise sovereign and the good general are able to strike and conquer... because they know what is essential."

Knowing what is essential requires detachment, not confidence.

AWH language:

Confidence without structure is noise.

Emotional Contamination and Visibility

Emotion pushes decisions into visibility prematurely.

Anger seeks confrontation.
Fear seeks reassurance.
Pride seeks recognition.

Each increases exposure.

Sun Tzu's preference for obscurity is psychological as much as tactical:

> "Appear weak when you are strong, and strong when
> you are weak."

This requires emotional discipline. It requires tolerating discomfort, misinterpretation, and delayed validation.

AWH principle:

Emotion demands visibility. Strategy avoids it.

Emotional Contamination Collapses Optionality

Emotion narrows choices.

It reframes:

- Delay as cowardice
- Restraint as weakness
- Reversal as failure

Sun Tzu repeatedly warns against desperation and rigidity:

> "Do not press a desperate foe too hard."

Desperation collapses options—for both sides.

AWH language:

> **Emotion turns flexible situations into forced ones.**

Emotional Decisions Override Cost Discipline

Emotion reorders cost logic.

Pride justifies expense.
Fear overpays for certainty.
Urgency ignores compounding loss.

Sun Tzu's constant emphasis on economy of force reflects his awareness of this failure mode.

> "The clever combatant looks to the effect of combined energy."

Combined energy is conserved energy. Emotion dissipates it.

Emotional Contamination and False Narratives

Emotion generates stories:

- "We had no choice."
- "We had to act."
- "This was necessary."

These narratives protect ego and suppress learning.

Sun Tzu does not tell stories. He gives conditions.

AWH language is direct:

> **If a decision requires a story to justify it, it probably violated the sequence.**

How Emotional Contamination Enters Organizations

Emotion is contagious.

One leader's fear becomes collective urgency.
One executive's pride becomes institutional escalation.
One team's anxiety becomes systemic overreaction.

Sun Tzu understood the danger of emotional transmission:

> "If words of command are not clear and distinct... the general is to blame."

Clarity suppresses emotional spread. Ambiguity amplifies it.

AWH principle:

> **Emotional discipline at the top is structural risk management.**

Detecting Emotional Contamination (Diagnostics)

Before any major decision, the framework requires interrogation of emotional state:

- Is this decision being made to relieve pressure?
- Are we responding to provocation or structure?

- Are we protecting reputation or position?
- Would we make the same decision if no one were watching?

If emotion is driving urgency, **stop**.

Sun Tzu's system assumes commanders can pause. Modern systems rarely allow it. That is why they fail more often.

Emotional Contamination vs. Moral Conviction

This chapter does not argue against values or ethics.

Sun Tzu was not immoral. He was **unsentimental**.

Ethical action does not require emotional escalation. It requires clarity of consequence.

AWH language draws the distinction:

> **Moral conviction without strategic discipline still produces unnecessary harm.**

Why Emotional Decisions Are Defended So Aggressively

Because they are identity-bound.

Challenging them feels like personal attack.
Reversing them feels like humiliation.

Sun Tzu avoids this by removing identity from strategy entirely.

AWH principle:

> **Detach the decision from the decider—or the decision will protect the decider at the expense of the outcome.**

Emotional Contamination and Post-Failure Rationalization

After failure, emotional decisions are often reframed as:

- "Unavoidable"
- "Principled"
- "Necessary"

Sun Tzu never excuses failure this way. He assumes error and corrects structure.

AWH language:

Countermeasure: Structural Discipline

The only reliable defense against emotional contamination is
sequence enforcement.

Sequence forces:

- Cost before justification
- Risk before courage
- Timing before urgency
- Restraint before action

Sun Tzu's entire system exists to impose this discipline.

Closing Orientation

This chapter identifies **emotional contamination** as the most
common failure mode in the entire framework.

Not because people are weak.
But because emotion is powerful—and strategy is fragile.

Sun Tzu did not trust emotion.
He trusted structure.

Ancient Wisdom Hacks makes this explicit:

If a decision feels obvious, urgent, and emotionally charged, it is probably wrong—or at least premature.

Clarity is quiet.
Discipline is unemotional.
Strategy survives only when emotion is subordinated to order.

That is not inhuman.

That is how humans avoid destroying themselves with their own intensity.

Chapter 15

Action Bias

Introduction: When Movement Replaces Thought

Modern strategy culture has a default setting: **act**.

If something feels uncertain, act.
If something feels threatening, act.
If something feels stalled, act.

Movement is treated as virtue. Stillness is treated as failure. In organizations, markets, politics, and leadership, action is praised reflexively—even when it worsens outcomes.

This bias is not accidental. It is cultural, psychological, and institutional. And it is one of the most reliable ways to break an otherwise sound decision system.

The Art of War is almost aggressively opposed to this instinct. Sun Tzu does not default to action. He defaults to *advantage*. Action appears only when advantage has already been secured.

This chapter examines **action bias** as a failure mode—how it distorts judgment, magnifies cost, and triggers escalation traps that are difficult or impossible to exit once entered.

The central warning of this chapter is simple:

**Movement is not progress.
Action is not strategy.**

Action Bias Defined

Action bias is the tendency to prefer doing something—anything—over doing nothing, even when restraint, delay, or non-decision would produce a better outcome.

It manifests as:

- Premature execution
- Overreaction to weak signals
- Continuous intervention
- Escalation to "show strength"

Action bias is rarely framed as recklessness. It is framed as leadership.

AWH language is blunt:

> **Action bias substitutes motion for structure and confuses effort with effectiveness.**

The Cultural Roots of Action Bias

Action bias is reinforced by culture at every level.

Organizational Culture

Organizations reward:

- Visible activity
- Responsiveness
- Quick decisions
- "Bias for action"

They rarely reward:

- Quiet restraint
- Waiting that avoids cost
- Non-decisions that preserve optionality

The result is predictable: leaders act to be seen acting.

Social and Psychological Reinforcement

Action produces:

- Relief from anxiety
- Social approval
- Narrative clarity

Inaction produces:

- Discomfort
- Criticism
- Ambiguity

Sun Tzu understood this psychological asymmetry and designed his system to counter it. His writing is deliberately unemotional, procedural, and unspectacular.

> "The general who wins a battle makes many calculations in his temple before the battle is fought."

Calculations are invisible. Battles are visible. Culture rewards the latter.

Mistaking Activity for Progress

One of the most destructive consequences of action bias is the **illusion of progress**.

Meetings are held.
Initiatives are launched.
Announcements are made.
Resources are mobilized.

Everything looks busy.

And nothing improves.

Sun Tzu never equates activity with advancement. He equates progress with *position*.

> "He who occupies the field of battle first and awaits his enemy is at ease."

Being "at ease" looks inactive. It is not. It is positional dominance.

AWH principle:

Progress is measured by reduced exposure, not increased motion.

Why Action Bias Feels Responsible

Action bias survives because it feels responsible.

Leaders say:

- "We had to do something."
- "Doing nothing wasn't an option."
- "At least we took action."

These statements protect identity, not outcomes.

Sun Tzu would reject them outright.

> "Move not unless you see an advantage; use not your troops unless there is something to be gained."

Action without advantage is not responsibility. It is **cost acceleration**.

AWH language is direct:

Responsibility is not acting.
Responsibility is preventing unnecessary loss.

Action Bias and Cost Amplification

Every action carries cost. Action bias multiplies those costs unnecessarily.

Costs amplified by action bias include:

- Direct expenditure
- Attention diversion
- Visibility-triggered resistance
- Commitment lock-in
- Opportunity destruction

Sun Tzu's warnings against prolonged warfare are warnings against action bias at scale.

> "There is no instance of a nation benefiting from prolonged warfare."

Prolongation often begins with a single unnecessary action—taken to appear decisive.

AWH principle:

> **Unnecessary action converts manageable situations into expensive ones.**

Action Bias and Information Distortion

Action bias distorts how information is interpreted.

Once action is taken:

- New information is filtered to justify the action
- Dissent is suppressed
- Reversal becomes costly

Sun Tzu avoids this trap by refusing to act until structure is secure.

> "If you know the enemy and know yourself, you need
> not fear the result of a hundred battles."

Knowing includes knowing *when not to commit.*

AWH language:

Action freezes interpretation.
Non-action keeps learning alive.

Escalation Traps: How Action Bias Locks You In

Escalation traps are the most dangerous outcome of action bias.

They follow a predictable pattern:

1. A small action is taken to resolve tension
2. The action triggers resistance or counteraction
3. More action is required to defend the first
4. Visibility increases
5. Exit costs rise

6. Commitment becomes identity-bound

Sun Tzu warns against this dynamic repeatedly, though implicitly.

> "Do not press a desperate foe too hard."

Why? Because desperation collapses choice. It forces terminal outcomes.

AWH language is explicit:

> **Most escalation traps begin with an unnecessary first move.**

Action Bias and Visibility Escalation

Action increases visibility. Visibility invites response.

Each response justifies further action.

Sun Tzu's preference for obscurity is designed to prevent this cascade.

> "When able to attack, we must seem unable; when using our forces, we must seem inactive."

Inactivity here is not weakness. It is **escalation avoidance**.

AWH principle:

**The first action often matters less than the
reaction it provokes.**

Action bias ignores this entirely.

The Myth of "We Can Always De-escalate"

Action bias is often defended with the claim that escalation can be reversed.

In reality:

- Visibility cannot be unseen
- Commitments cannot be unmade cheaply
- Narratives cannot be retracted
- Trust cannot be restored instantly

Sun Tzu never assumes reversibility after action. He assumes **consequences persist**.

AWH language:

**De-escalation is harder than non-escalation.
Do not enter what you cannot easily exit.**

Action Bias vs. Strategic Initiative

Action bias is often confused with initiative.

They are not the same.

- **Action bias**: moving to feel in control
- **Strategic initiative**: forcing others to respond

Sun Tzu prizes the latter and avoids the former.

> "If the enemy is taking his ease, give him no rest."

Note: this does not require visible action. Pressure can be applied structurally—through positioning, denial, and patience.

AWH reframes initiative:

> **True initiative is making others move while you remain optional.**

Action bias does the opposite.

Action Bias and Leadership Theater

Many actions exist primarily to be seen.

They are symbolic, performative, or narrative-driven.

Sun Tzu has no patience for leadership theater.

"The general who is skilled in defense hides in the most secret recesses of the earth."

Hidden defense does not photograph well. It works anyway.

AWH language is blunt:

If an action exists mainly to signal leadership, it is probably not strategic.

Action Bias and Ego Reinforcement

Action bias feeds ego.

Acting confirms:

- Authority
- Relevance
- Identity

Not acting invites doubt.

Sun Tzu repeatedly warns against ego-driven decisions:

"The general who is choleric and quick-tempered may be provoked by insults."

Provocation succeeds only when ego demands response.

AWH principle:

Ego converts restraint into perceived weakness—and action into self-harm.

Action Bias and Resource Exhaustion

Continuous action exhausts systems.

Teams burn out.
Capital depletes.
Attention fragments.

Sun Tzu emphasizes endurance over momentum.

"In war, discipline is more important than numbers."

Discipline includes **knowing when not to act**.

AWH language:

Systems fail not from one bad action, but from too many unnecessary ones.

The Counterintuitive Advantage of Stillness

Stillness is uncomfortable—but powerful.

It:

- Preserves resources
- Forces others to reveal intent
- Prevents escalation
- Maintains optionality

Sun Tzu's system relies on stillness more than movement.

> "He who is prudent and lies in wait for an enemy who is not, will be victorious."

Waiting is not absence of strategy. It is **strategy expressed through restraint**.

Diagnosing Action Bias in Real Time

Before any action, this framework demands interrogation:

- Are we acting to reduce cost—or to relieve pressure?
- Does this action improve position—or merely create activity?
- What reaction will this provoke?
- Can we afford the escalation path this opens?

If these questions cannot be answered, **do not act**.

Action Bias vs. Prepared Action

This chapter does not argue against action itself.

Prepared action—taken after sequence, preparation, and restraint—is decisive and efficient.

Sun Tzu allows speed only after structure is secure:

> "Let your rapidity be that of the wind."

AWH principle:

> **Action is powerful only when it ends something—not when it starts a chain reaction.**

Why Action Bias Persists Despite Evidence

Because:

- It is socially rewarded
- It feels good
- It creates narrative closure
- It protects identity

Sun Tzu's work persists because it refuses all four.

AWH language is unsentimental:

> **Strategy is not therapy.**
> **It does not exist to make you feel effective.**

Breaking the Action Bias

The only reliable antidote to action bias is **sequence discipline**.

- Cost before movement
- Risk before courage
- Timing before urgency
- Restraint before action

Sun Tzu built his entire system around this ordering.

Closing Orientation

This chapter identifies **action bias** as a systemic failure mode—not a personality flaw.

Action bias breaks strategy by:

- Mistaking motion for progress
- Converting pressure into escalation
- Locking systems into costly paths

Sun Tzu did not win by acting more.
He won by **acting less—and only when action resolved rather than multiplied conflict**.

Ancient Wisdom Hacks makes the discipline explicit:

If action does not clearly reduce total cost, it is probably feeding bias—not strategy.

Stillness is not weakness.
Restraint is not delay.
And the most dangerous action is often the first unnecessary one.

Understanding that truth is the difference between control and collapse.

Chapter 16

Overexposure

Introduction: The Moment Strategy Becomes Targetable

Most strategic failures do not begin with a bad idea.
They begin with **being seen too soon**.

Intent is revealed before it is protected.
Signals are sent before they are supported.
Commitments are made before costs are controlled.

From that moment forward, the system changes. What was once optional becomes reactive. What was once flexible becomes rigid. What was once private becomes contested.

The Art of War treats exposure as danger by default. Sun Tzu does not ask whether visibility can be managed later. He assumes that once exposure occurs, **counteraction follows**—predictably and relentlessly.

This chapter examines **overexposure** as a failure mode: how revealing intent too early, signaling before preparation, and committing publicly before cost control destroys leverage and forces escalation.

The governing principle is uncompromising:

Overexposure Defined

Overexposure occurs when information about intent, capability, timing, or commitment becomes visible **before** the system is prepared to absorb the consequences.

It is not simply visibility.
It is **premature visibility**.

Overexposure includes:

- Announcing plans before readiness
- Signaling strength without backing structure
- Public commitments that remove exit paths
- Transparency that benefits observers more than actors

AWH language is direct:

> **Overexposure is not honesty.**
> **It is structural negligence.**

Why Exposure Changes the Game

Before exposure, decisions occur in a private decision space.

After exposure:

- Others adapt
- Resistance forms
- Countermeasures appear
- Costs rise

Sun Tzu assumes this dynamic everywhere.

> "If the enemy leaves a door open, you must rush in."

Visibility creates doors—for others.

AWH principle:

> **Exposure accelerates the opponent's decision cycle, not yours.**

Once exposed, you are no longer choosing freely. You are responding.

Revealing Intent Too Early

Intent is the most sensitive strategic variable.

It answers:

- What you want
- Where you are going
- What you value
- What you will defend

Revealing intent early gives others time to:

- Block
- Preempt
- Undermine
- Reprice risk

Sun Tzu treats intent as something to be masked until action is unavoidable.

> "When able to attack, we must seem unable."

This is not deception for its own sake. It is **intent protection**.

AWH language is precise:

> **Intent revealed before leverage is built becomes a liability.**

Why Early Intent Disclosure Feels Virtuous

Modern cultures praise transparency.

They equate openness with trust, leadership, and confidence. This framing is naïve in adversarial or competitive environments.

Transparency feels virtuous because:

- It reduces internal tension
- It creates alignment narratives
- It signals confidence

Sun Tzu would reject all three as irrelevant to outcome.

AWH principle:

> **Virtue signaling that increases exposure is not leadership.**

Signaling Before Preparation

Signals are promises.

They imply:

- Capability
- Readiness
- Willingness to act

When signals are sent before preparation, they invite tests.

Sun Tzu understands signaling as a weapon that must be used sparingly:

> "Appear weak when you are strong, and strong when you are weak."

Signaling strength without preparation is provocation. It dares others to challenge you before you are ready.

AWH language:

**A signal without structure is a dare, not a
deterrent.**

The Testing Effect

One of the least understood consequences of overexposure is
testing.

When intent or commitment is visible:

- Others probe boundaries
- Minor challenges escalate
- Weakness is sought deliberately

Sun Tzu assumes this behavior is inevitable.

> "If the enemy is taking his ease, give him no rest."

Others will test visible positions. If preparation is incomplete, those
tests become breaches.

AWH principle:

> **Visibility invites testing; preparation determines
> the outcome.**

Public Commitment Before Cost Control

Public commitment is irreversible signaling.

It converts:

- Options into obligations
- Flexibility into reputation risk
- Reconsideration into humiliation

Sun Tzu avoids public commitment entirely.

He does not announce campaigns.
He does not publish intent.
He does not bind himself rhetorically before binding conditions structurally.

AWH language is blunt:

> **Public commitment before cost control is gambling with reputation and resources simultaneously.**

Why Public Commitment Is So Dangerous

Public commitments:

- Raise exit costs
- Invite opposition coordination
- Force escalation to avoid embarrassment
- Convert sunk cost into identity defense

Once a commitment is public, the decision is no longer evaluated on merit—it is defended on pride.

Sun Tzu rejects this entirely:

> "The supreme art of war is to subdue the enemy without fighting."

Public commitments make non-fighting politically impossible.

Overexposure and Escalation Traps

Overexposure is one of the fastest paths into escalation traps.

The sequence is predictable:

1. Intent is revealed early
2. Opposition mobilizes
3. Initial resistance appears
4. Commitment must be defended
5. More resources are deployed
6. Exit becomes reputationally costly

Sun Tzu warns against this dynamic implicitly through his aversion to siege warfare.

"If you lay siege to a town, you will exhaust your strength."

Siege is what happens when exposure forces confrontation that could have been avoided.

AWH principle:

Overexposure turns avoidable conflict into unavoidable escalation.

Overexposure Collapses Optionality

Optionality depends on ambiguity.

Ambiguity allows:

- Delay
- Adjustment
- Reversal
- Quiet exit

Exposure collapses ambiguity.

Sun Tzu prizes ambiguity relentlessly.

"Be subtle! Be subtle! And use your spies for every kind of business."

Subtlety is optionality preservation.

AWH language:

Once exposed, every future move is interpreted through the lens of that exposure.

Overexposure and Timing Destruction

Timing is fragile.

It requires:

- Control of information
- Freedom from pressure
- Ability to wait

Overexposure destroys timing by creating urgency—externally and internally.

Sun Tzu's discipline depends on timing control:

> "He will win who knows when to fight and when not to fight."

Once exposed, timing decisions are no longer yours alone.

AWH principle:

Exposure hands timing leverage to others.

The Illusion of "Owning the Narrative"

Overexposure is often justified by narrative control.

"We need to get ahead of it."
"We need to set expectations."
"We need to shape perception."

Sun Tzu does not care about narratives. He cares about **position**.

Narratives are fragile. Positions are durable.

AWH language is explicit:

> **If your strategy depends on narrative control, it is already exposed.**

Overexposure and Information Asymmetry Loss

Before exposure, you know more than others.

After exposure, that asymmetry collapses.

Sun Tzu treats information asymmetry as decisive:

> "What enables the wise sovereign and the good general to strike and conquer... is foreknowledge."

Foreknowledge loses value when intent is public.

AWH principle:

**Information advantage dies the moment intent is
revealed.**

Why Leaders Overexpose Anyway

Because overexposure:

- Feels decisive
- Signals confidence
- Creates alignment
- Relieves internal pressure

These are psychological benefits—not strategic ones.

Sun Tzu designs his system to deny psychological comfort in
exchange for structural advantage.

AWH language is blunt:

**Overexposure is often chosen because it feels like
leadership.**

It is not.

Overexposure in Organizations

In organizations, overexposure appears as:

- Premature roadmaps
- Public deadlines without buffers
- Announced strategies before capability
- Visible pivots before cost is known

Each creates internal and external pressure that distorts execution.

Sun Tzu's emphasis on discipline and clarity is designed to prevent this.

> "If orders are not clear and distinct... the general is to blame."

Clarity does not require publicity.

Overexposure and Ego Binding

Once exposed, leaders become emotionally bound to outcomes.

Reversal becomes personal.
Adjustment becomes embarrassment.
Restraint becomes weakness.

Sun Tzu avoids ego binding by avoiding exposure.

AWH principle:

Exposure ties identity to decisions.
Strategy requires the opposite.

When Exposure Is Acceptable

This chapter does not argue for permanent obscurity.

Exposure can be useful **after** conditions are secured.

Exposure is acceptable when:

- Cost is controlled
- Risk is bounded
- Preparation is complete
- Timing favors you
- Counteraction is survivable

Sun Tzu allows visibility only when advantage is irreversible.

"Let your rapidity be that of the wind."

Speed and exposure are safe only when resistance is already neutralized.

Exposure as a Deliberate Trade

Exposure should be **spent**, not indulged.

Before increasing visibility, the framework demands answers:

1. What advantage does exposure create now?
2. What resistance will it trigger?
3. What optionality will it destroy?
4. Can we absorb the resulting pressure?
5. Is there a cheaper way to achieve the same effect?

If these cannot be answered, exposure is premature.

Diagnostic: Are We Overexposed?

Warning signs include:

- Public commitment without exit clauses
- Announcements preceding preparation
- Pressure to "be seen doing something"
- Decisions defended by reputation rather than outcome

Sun Tzu's system exists to catch these signs early.

Overexposure vs. Transparency

This chapter is not an argument against honesty.

It is an argument against **unnecessary disclosure in adversarial contexts**.

Sun Tzu is not dishonest. He is disciplined.

AWH language:

> **Transparency inside trust boundaries is strength.
> Transparency outside them is exposure.**

Overexposure and Failure Amplification

When exposed systems fail, failure is amplified.

Mistakes become signals.
Weakness becomes contagious.
Recovery becomes harder.

Sun Tzu avoids this by avoiding exposure until outcomes are secured.

AWH principle:

> **Exposure magnifies both success and
> failure—never expose before success is likely.**

Closing Orientation

This chapter establishes **overexposure** as one of the most costly and irreversible failure modes in strategy.

Not because visibility is evil.
But because **premature visibility is expensive**.

Sun Tzu did not win by declaring intent.
He won by **arriving prepared at moments when intent no longer mattered**.

Ancient Wisdom Hacks makes the discipline explicit:

> **Do not ask, "Should we be transparent?"**
> **Ask, "Who benefits from this visibility—and who pays for it?"**

If the answer is unclear, remain obscure.

Strategy works best when it is understood **after** it has already succeeded.

Chapter 17

Victory Myopia

Introduction: When Winning Becomes the Problem

Not all failures look like defeats.

Some look like victories.

Objectives are achieved.
Opponents are pushed back.
Metrics turn green.
Applause follows.

And yet—months or years later—the position is weaker, options are narrower, and costs are higher than before the "win."

This is **victory myopia**: the inability to see beyond the immediate engagement to the structural consequences that follow.

The Art of War is relentlessly hostile to this kind of thinking. Sun Tzu does not define success as winning battles. He defines it as **preserving advantage while minimizing cost across time**.

> "To fight and conquer in all your battles is not supreme excellence; supreme excellence consists in breaking the enemy's resistance without fighting."

This line is not anti-combat rhetoric. It is a warning: **winning visible contests can conceal deeper strategic failure**.

This chapter examines how tactical success masks long-term damage, how short-term wins erode position, and why many organizations, leaders, and states lose *after* they have already won.

Victory Myopia Defined

Victory myopia occurs when decision-makers:

- Evaluate success at the engagement level instead of the system level
- Optimize for immediate outcomes instead of future position
- Confuse winning with progress
- Ignore second- and third-order consequences

It is not ignorance.
It is **misplaced focus**.

AWH language is precise:

> **Victory myopia is success measured too narrowly and too soon.**

The result is a paradoxical failure mode: the better you appear to be doing, the worse your underlying position becomes.

Winning the Engagement, Losing the Position

Engagements are local.
Positions are systemic.

An engagement is a moment.
A position is a trajectory.

Sun Tzu never evaluates success by isolated encounters. He evaluates it by posture, endurance, and optionality.

> "In war, then, let your great object be victory, not lengthy campaigns."

Lengthy campaigns often begin with tactical wins that encourage further engagement rather than consolidation.

AWH reframes this distinction:

> **An engagement answers, "Did we win this exchange?"**
> **A position answers, "Are we stronger after this than before?"**

Victory myopia answers only the first question.

How Tactical Success Masks Strategic Failure

Tactical success produces immediate feedback:

- Numbers improve
- Resistance retreats
- Authority is reinforced

Strategic failure produces delayed feedback:

- Optionality erodes
- Costs compound
- Dependencies increase
- Exposure rises

Because humans overweight immediate feedback, tactical success is trusted more than structural warning signs.

Sun Tzu understood this bias implicitly. That is why he avoids language of heroism or triumph and focuses instead on conditions.

> "The general who wins a battle makes many calculations in his temple before the battle is fought."

The calculations are not about *winning the battle*. They are about **what the battle does to the system afterward**.

AWH principle:

> **If a win creates conditions that require more wins to survive, it was not a strategic success.**

The Trap of Metrics and Scoreboards

Victory myopia thrives in metric-driven environments.

Metrics reward:

- Speed
- Volume
- Output
- Visible results

They rarely capture:

- Optionality loss
- Reputation damage
- Escalation risk
- Long-term fragility

Sun Tzu never counts victories. He counts sustainability.

> "There is no instance of a nation benefiting from prolonged warfare."

Prolongation is often justified by early wins that look good on paper.

AWH language:

Metrics that reward engagement often punish position—just slowly enough to be ignored.

Short-Term Wins That Create Long-Term Damage

Victory myopia appears in predictable patterns across domains.

Business

- Aggressive pricing wins market share but destroys margins
- Rapid expansion wins headlines but collapses execution
- Public commitments drive momentum but lock in cost

Leadership

- Decisive intervention resolves conflict but undermines authority
- Visible control restores order but kills initiative
- "Strong" responses deter dissent but increase quiet resistance

Conflict and Negotiation

- Hardline stances win concessions but poison future leverage
- Escalation forces retreat but invites counter-escalation
- Public victories humiliate opponents and harden opposition

Sun Tzu warns against all of these implicitly.

> "Do not press a desperate foe too hard."

Why? Because humiliation converts temporary defeat into permanent hostility.

AWH principle:

A win that creates resentment is a loan at compounding interest.

Victory Myopia and Cost Blindness

Tactical victories often hide cost by deferring it.

Costs pushed forward include:

- Maintenance burden
- Reputation repair
- Defensive spending
- Emotional exhaustion

Because these costs are delayed, they are discounted at the moment of victory.

Sun Tzu refuses to discount cost.

> "If you lay siege to a town, you will exhaust your strength."

Siege can succeed tactically and still fail strategically.

AWH language:

**If a victory increases your cost of staying in place,
it is not a gain.**

Why Victory Myopia Feels Rational

Victory myopia is reinforced by social validation.

Wins are celebrated.
Victors are promoted.
Results are praised.

The damage is invisible until it is irreversible.

Sun Tzu avoids this trap by removing personal reward from the
evaluation of success. He does not ask who looks strong. He asks
who survives intact.

AWH principle:

> **What feels like success under applause often fails
> under time.**

The Escalation Effect of Tactical Wins

One of the most dangerous consequences of victory myopia is
escalation.

A tactical win often:

- Raises expectations
- Forces repetition
- Increases visibility
- Demands defense

Each subsequent engagement becomes harder and more expensive.

Sun Tzu avoids escalation through restraint and obscurity.

> "To subdue the enemy without fighting is the acme of skill."

AWH reframes this:

> **The best victories reduce the need for future victories.**

If a win creates a requirement to keep winning just to hold position, the system is already failing.

Winning Changes Behavior—Often for the Worse

Victories alter decision behavior.

They:

- Increase confidence
- Reduce caution

- Encourage shortcuts
- Normalize overreach

Sun Tzu is aware of this danger and emphasizes discipline over momentum.

"In war, discipline is more important than numbers."

Discipline prevents success from eroding judgment.

AWH language:

Unexamined success is one of the fastest paths to strategic decay.

Victory Myopia and Visibility

Victories increase visibility.

Visibility:

- Attracts challengers
- Invites testing
- Forces signaling

Sun Tzu prefers invisible advantage to visible triumph.

"The general who is skilled in defense hides in the most secret recesses of the earth."

AWH principle:

Visible victories invite invisible costs.

The Difference Between Winning and Resolving

Winning answers *who prevailed*.
Resolving answers *whether the issue is finished*.

Many victories do not resolve anything. They merely pause conflict at higher cost.

Sun Tzu is explicit about resolution:

> "In war, then, let your great object be victory, not lengthy campaigns."

Victory here means **ending the conflict**, not scoring points.

AWH language:

> **A victory that does not reduce future conflict is incomplete.**

Victory Myopia and Identity Binding

Victories bind identity.

Leaders become associated with wins.
Reversal becomes personal.
Adaptation becomes betrayal of narrative.

Sun Tzu avoids identity binding by never personalizing success.

AWH principle:

> **When identity attaches to victory, strategy becomes theater.**

The need to preserve a winning image often prevents necessary course correction.

How Victory Myopia Breaks the Decision Sequence

Victory myopia reorders the canonical sequence:

- Action is justified by success
- Cost is ignored because "it worked"
- Risk is dismissed due to confidence
- Restraint is abandoned

Each violation compounds the next.

Sun Tzu never allows success to override sequence.

Diagnostic: Is This Victory Making Us Weaker?

After any apparent win, the framework requires interrogation:

- Did this reduce total cost—or defer it?
- Did optionality increase or decrease?
- Did visibility rise without compensation?
- Did we resolve the issue or entrench it?
- Are we freer now—or more committed?

If answers trend negative, the victory is suspect.

When Losing Is Strategically Superior to Winning

This is one of the hardest truths in strategy.

Sometimes not winning an engagement:

- Preserves ambiguity
- Avoids escalation
- Maintains leverage
- Allows repositioning

Sun Tzu accepts this without hesitation.

> "If the enemy is in superior strength, evade him."

Evading is not losing. It is **declining a costly win**.

AWH language:

> **A refused victory can be a strategic success.**

Victory Myopia in Organizations

In organizations, victory myopia appears as:

- Celebrating launches instead of outcomes
- Rewarding speed over sustainability
- Promoting fire-fighters instead of architects
- Confusing crisis resolution with progress

Sun Tzu's system would reject all of these incentives.

The Discipline of Post-Victory Restraint

True strategic discipline is tested **after** success, not before it.

After victory, restraint must:

- Reassert sequence
- Re-evaluate cost
- Re-bound risk
- Reduce visibility

Sun Tzu's aversion to prolonged warfare is post-victory discipline.

AWH principle:

> **What you do after winning determines whether you actually won.**

Why Victory Myopia Persists

Because:

- It feels good
- It is rewarded
- It simplifies narratives
- It delays accountability

Sun Tzu's work persists because it refuses all four.

Closing Orientation

This chapter identifies **victory myopia** as a subtle but devastating failure mode.

Not because winning is bad.
But because **winning the wrong thing at the wrong level is indistinguishable from losing—just slower.**

Sun Tzu did not pursue victories.
He pursued **positions that made victory unnecessary**.

Ancient Wisdom Hacks makes the discipline explicit:

> **If a victory makes the next decision harder, it was not a strategic success.**

True strategy does not ask, *Did we win?*
It asks, *Are we stronger, freer, and less exposed than before?*

Anything else is illusion—paid for later, at full price.

PART V

APPLICATION WITHOUT TACTICS

(How this framework is used without collapsing into advice)

Chapter 18

Applying the Framework Across Domains

Introduction: Why This Chapter Refuses to Give Advice

Most strategy books fail at the moment they attempt to be helpful.

They move from principle to prescription.
They convert structure into tips.
They trade discipline for examples that feel actionable.

That is precisely what this framework will **not** do.

This chapter applies the framework across domains **without collapsing it into tactics**. There are no playbooks, no checklists disguised as advice, and no domain-specific tricks. Instead, this chapter demonstrates how the **same decision sequence** governs radically different environments—while remaining unchanged itself.

The Art of War does the same. Sun Tzu never gives you instructions for your specific war. He gives you a system that survives every war.

> "There are not more than five musical notes, yet the combinations of these five give rise to more melodies than can ever be heard."

The system adapts.
The sequence does not.

That is the governing rule of this chapter:

The framework adapts; the sequence does not.

Why Application Without Tactics Is Necessary

Tactics decay.

They age with technology.
They fail across contexts.
They invite imitation.

Frameworks endure.

They remain valid when:

- Conditions change
- Environments shift
- Incentives invert
- Technology disrupts

Sun Tzu understood this asymmetry. That is why *The Art of War* contains almost no tactics and remains relevant across millennia.

AWH language is explicit:

> **If a strategy requires tactics to function, it is already obsolete.**

This chapter demonstrates application by **mapping decision primitives**, not by prescribing moves.

The Canonical Sequence (Reasserted)

Before entering domains, the order must be restated—because this chapter assumes it silently at all times:

1. Assess constraint
2. Identify cost
3. Bound risk
4. Evaluate timing
5. Prepare position
6. Control visibility
7. Apply restraint

8. Act only if action reduces total cost

This sequence is not contextual.
It is not optional.
It is not adaptive.

Only the *inputs* change.

Domain 1: Business Acquisition

Business acquisition is one of the most emotionally and cognitively contaminated decision environments in existence.

It combines:

- Financial leverage
- Ego and identity
- Time pressure
- Narrative temptation
- Asymmetric information

Most acquisition failures are not caused by bad valuation models. They are caused by **sequence violation**.

Constraint

Constraints include:

- Capital limits
- Regulatory boundaries

- Operator capability
- Market structure

Acquisitions fail when buyers treat ambition as a variable rather than a constraint.

Sun Tzu opens his work with constraint framing for a reason.

> "War is a matter of vital importance to the State… the road to survival or ruin."

Acquisition is the same.

AWH principle:

> **If the acquisition requires you to become someone else to survive it, the constraint has already been violated.**

Cost

Cost is not purchase price.

It includes:

- Integration burden
- Management attention
- Opportunity cost
- Reputation exposure
- Exit friction

Victory myopia is common here: deals "win" on paper while destroying future optionality.

AWH language:

> **If owning the asset costs more than not owning it—over time—the deal is already negative.**

Risk

Risk is not variance in return.
It is exposure to irreversible loss.

Examples:

- Platform dependency
- Legal entanglement
- Cultural incompatibility
- Capital lock-in

Sun Tzu never evaluates upside without survivability.

> "If you know yourself but not the enemy, for every victory gained you will also suffer a defeat."

In acquisitions, the "enemy" is often hidden structure.

Timing

The best acquisition opportunities often emerge **when others are forced to sell**, not when buyers feel confident.

Urgency usually favors the seller.

AWH language:

> **If the deal requires urgency to close, timing is probably wrong.**

Preparation

Preparation includes:

- Operational shadowing
- Scenario stress-testing
- Exit modeling
- Control mapping

Prepared buyers rarely feel excited. They feel bored.

That boredom is the signal.

Visibility

Public deal chatter attracts:

- Competing bidders
- Regulatory scrutiny
- Seller leverage

Sun Tzu would never announce intent before control.

> "When able to attack, we must seem unable."

Restraint

Many acquisitions should not be made.

Restraint here preserves capital, attention, and identity.

AWH language:

The best acquisition is often the one not pursued.

Action

Action is justified only when:

- Cost is controlled
- Risk is bounded
- Timing favors the buyer
- Exit remains viable

Anything else is gambling with leverage.

Domain 2: Leadership Decisions

Leadership decisions are rarely tactical. They are **structural signals**.

They affect:

- Morale
- Incentives
- Authority boundaries
- Cultural memory

Most leadership failures come from **action bias** and **overexposure**.

Constraint

Constraints include:

- Organizational maturity
- Talent depth
- Trust capital
- Institutional memory

Leaders who ignore constraint resort to force.

Sun Tzu avoids this entirely.

> "If soldiers are punished before they have grown attached to you, they will not prove submissive."

Cost

Leadership costs include:

- Credibility erosion
- Decision fatigue
- Culture damage
- Silent disengagement

AWH language:

The cost of a leadership decision is often paid by people who never speak again.

Risk

Risk includes:

- Precedent creation
- Authority dilution
- Retaliatory compliance

Once a leadership move is made, it becomes part of the system.

Timing

Intervening too early trains dependency.
Intervening too late trains decay.

Timing in leadership is about **signal maturity**, not urgency.

Preparation

Prepared leaders:

- Define thresholds
- Pre-communicate principles
- Align authority quietly

Unprepared leaders improvise publicly.

Visibility

Visible leadership action invites:

- Performance theater
- Political alignment
- Surface compliance

Sun Tzu prefers quiet order.

> "The general who is skilled in defense hides in the most secret recesses of the earth."

Restraint

Many leadership problems resolve themselves if not prematurely escalated.

AWH principle:

Intervention should be rare enough that it still works.

Action

Leadership action is valid only if it:

- Reduces future intervention
- Clarifies structure
- Preserves trust

Otherwise, it trains dependence.

Domain 3: Competitive Environments

Competition tempts escalation.

It rewards visibility, speed, and aggression—often at long-term cost.

Sun Tzu treats competition as a positioning problem, not a fighting problem.

Constraint

Constraints include:

- Market structure
- Switching costs
- Capital asymmetry
- Regulatory environment

Many competitive "moves" are impossible regardless of intelligence.

Cost

Competitive cost includes:

- Price erosion
- Brand damage
- Retaliation cycles

Winning market share can destroy profit.

Victory myopia thrives here.

Risk

Risk includes:

- Escalation loops
- Dependency creation
- Strategic exhaustion

Sun Tzu avoids drawn-out conflict for this reason.

Timing

Entering competition at the wrong moment invites entrenchment.

Waiting allows others to overextend.

> "He who is prudent and lies in wait for an enemy who
> is not, will be victorious."

Preparation

Preparation includes:

- Supply chain resilience
- Defensive moats
- Cost buffers

Prepared competitors rarely need to signal.

Visibility

Competitive signaling accelerates response.

AWH language:

> **The competitor you announce yourself to is
> already adapting.**

Restraint

Not every competitive challenge deserves response.

Ignoring provocation often forces others to spend energy alone.

Action

Competitive action should **end something**, not begin a cycle.

If retaliation is guaranteed, action should be reconsidered.

Domain 4: Personal Authority

Personal authority is not dominance.
It is **credibility under restraint**.

Most people lose authority by trying to assert it.

Sun Tzu never advocates assertion.

Constraint

Constraints include:

- Role
- Reputation
- Social capital
- Dependency structure

Authority cannot exceed trust.

Cost

Cost includes:

- Reputation loss
- Emotional exhaustion
- Escalation pressure

Public "wins" often damage long-term authority.

Risk

Risk includes:

- Being challenged publicly
- Forcing escalation
- Losing ambiguity

Authority thrives on ambiguity.

Timing

Correct timing in personal authority often means **not responding**.

Silence forces others to reveal intent.

Preparation

Preparation includes:

- Boundary clarity
- Value consistency
- Quiet alignment

Prepared authority does not need to perform.

Visibility

Visibility invites testing.

AWH language:

Authority that must be announced is already weak.

Restraint

Restraint is the foundation of authority.

It signals confidence without exposure.

Action

Action is reserved for moments when:

- Boundaries must be reset
- Structure must be clarified
- Future cost is reduced

Anything else is ego defense.

Domain 5: Strategic Withdrawal

Withdrawal is the most stigmatized strategic act—and one of the most misunderstood.

Sun Tzu treats withdrawal as intelligence, not defeat.

> "If the enemy is in superior strength, evade him."

Constraint

Constraints include:

- Asymmetry
- Exhaustion
- Resource depletion

Ignoring these makes withdrawal inevitable—but later and costlier.

Cost

Staying has cost.
Leaving has cost.

The question is **which compounds faster**.

Risk

Risk includes:

- Escalation
- Identity binding
- Terminal loss

Withdrawal preserves survivability.

Timing

Early withdrawal preserves optionality.
Late withdrawal destroys it.

Preparation

Prepared withdrawal includes:

- Narrative insulation
- Resource staging
- Position repositioning

Unprepared withdrawal becomes collapse.

Visibility

Quiet exits preserve dignity and leverage.

Public exits invite humiliation and pursuit.

Restraint

Restraint prevents staying past the point of advantage.

Action

Withdrawal is action when it reduces total cost.

Anything else is stubbornness.

Why the Sequence Never Changes

Across all domains:

- Constraints differ
- Costs differ
- Risks differ
- Signals differ

But **order does not**.

Sun Tzu never adapts sequence to context. He adapts interpretation.

AWH language states it plainly:

> **The framework adapts; the sequence does not.**

Any system that allows reordering under pressure will fail under pressure.

Closing Orientation

This chapter demonstrates that the framework does not tell you **what to do**.

It tells you **how to decide**.

That distinction is everything.

Sun Tzu did not win wars by giving advice.
He won by enforcing order in decision-making.

Ancient Wisdom Hacks makes this explicit:

> **If you need tactics to apply this framework, you are already misusing it.**

Strategy survives by structure, not instruction.
And the structure does not bend—only the context does.

That is why this system endures.

Chapter 19

Reading Conditions, Not Situations

Introduction: Why Most Strategic Analysis Is Performed at the Wrong Level

Most people believe they are analyzing reality.

They are not.

They are analyzing **situations**.

Situations are what is visible:

- Events
- Crises
- Headlines
- Conversations
- Discrete problems demanding response

Situations feel concrete. They feel urgent. They feel actionable.

And they are almost always misleading.

The Art of War does not analyze situations. Sun Tzu analyzes **conditions**—the underlying forces that make outcomes inevitable long before situations appear dramatic.

This chapter formalizes one of the most critical distinctions in the entire framework:

> **Situations are surface-level.**
> **Conditions determine outcome.**

If you respond to situations, you will always be late.
If you diagnose conditions, you often do not need to respond at all.

Situations: The Theater of Strategy

Situations are what draw attention.

They include:

- A sudden crisis
- A hostile move by a competitor
- A leadership conflict
- A market shift
- A public confrontation

Situations demand explanation. They invite reaction. They generate stories.

That is why humans fixate on them.

But situations are **expressions**, not causes.

Sun Tzu never begins analysis with events. He begins with structure.

"The general who wins a battle makes many calculations in his temple before the battle is fought."

The battle is the situation.
The calculations diagnose the conditions that made the battle's outcome predictable.

AWH language is blunt:

Situations are noise amplified by visibility.
Conditions are signal hidden beneath it.

Why Situations Are So Persuasive

Situations dominate attention because they:

- Trigger emotion
- Create urgency
- Demand response
- Appear novel

Conditions, by contrast, are:

- Slow-moving
- Unphotogenic
- Repetitive
- Often boring

This asymmetry creates a systematic analytical failure: decision-makers react to what is loud instead of what is decisive.

Sun Tzu designs his entire system to counter this bias.

> "He who exercises no forethought but makes light of
> his opponents is sure to be captured by them."

Forethought is condition analysis. Reactivity is situation response.

Conditions Defined

Conditions are the **persistent structural realities** that govern outcomes regardless of intent.

They include:

- Incentive structures
- Resource asymmetries
- Information flow
- Fatigue and morale
- Time pressure
- Visibility dynamics
- Optionality distribution

Conditions exist before situations arise and persist after they resolve.

AWH definition:

> **Conditions are what make some actions cheap,
> others expensive, and some impossible.**

Situations merely reveal which conditions are already dominant.

The Core Error: Treating Situations as Causes

One of the most destructive analytical mistakes is treating situations as causal.

Examples:

- "This failed because of a bad decision."
- "This conflict started because of that comment."
- "The deal collapsed because negotiations broke down."

These explanations are emotionally satisfying—and structurally false.

Sun Tzu never explains outcomes this way.

He attributes failure to misalignment with conditions.

> "If you know the enemy and know yourself, you need not fear the result of a hundred battles."

Knowing here means knowing **conditions**, not events.

AWH language:

> **Events do not cause failure.**
> **They expose it.**

Situations Are Stories; Conditions Are Systems

Situations lend themselves to narrative.

They have:

- Beginnings
- Turning points
- Culprits
- Climaxes

Conditions do not.

Conditions are systemic. They lack protagonists. They do not resolve cleanly. They persist.

This creates a strong bias toward story-based analysis.

Sun Tzu rejects stories entirely. His work contains almost no narrative.

Why?

Because stories personalize what is structural and obscure what is inevitable.

AWH principle:

Frameworks diagnose conditions, not stories.

Stories explain how something felt.
Conditions explain why it happened.

Reading Conditions: What Sun Tzu Actually Does

Sun Tzu's famous "five constant factors" are not situational variables. They are **condition categories**:

- Moral influence (alignment and morale)
- Heaven (timing, seasonality, cycles)
- Earth (terrain, positioning, constraints)
- The Commander (discipline, temperament)
- Method and discipline (systems, logistics)

None of these describe an event. They describe **operating conditions**.

> "These five heads should be familiar to every general."

Why? Because they determine outcomes *before* contact.

AWH reframes this:

> **If conditions are unfavorable, no situational brilliance will save you.**
> **If conditions are favorable, situations resolve themselves.**

Why Situational Excellence Often Fails

Many people are excellent at handling situations.

They:

- Speak well under pressure
- Improvise convincingly
- Make quick decisions
- Project confidence

And still fail.

Why?

Because situational skill cannot overcome hostile conditions.

Sun Tzu never praises improvisation under fire. He praises preparation that makes improvisation unnecessary.

> "Victorious warriors win first and then go to war."

Winning first means **engineering conditions** that remove dependence on situational brilliance.

AWH language:

> **If success depends on how well you perform in the moment, the conditions are already against you.**

Conditions Make Outcomes Predictable

One of the uncomfortable truths of strategy is that outcomes are often predictable long before they occur.

Not because of clairvoyance.
But because conditions constrain possible futures.

Examples:

- An exhausted team will eventually fracture
- A leveraged business will eventually lose flexibility
- A visible strategy will eventually attract opposition
- A prolonged conflict will eventually consume resources

Sun Tzu treats these as axioms, not guesses.

> "There is no instance of a nation benefiting from prolonged warfare."

This is not historical commentary. It is condition analysis.

AWH principle:

Conditions do not care about intent, talent, or optimism.

Situations Create Pressure to Decide; Conditions Determine Whether You Should

Situations demand decisions.

Conditions determine whether decisions are necessary—or whether waiting is superior.

Sun Tzu consistently prioritizes the latter.

> "He who is prudent and lies in wait for an enemy who is not, will be victorious."

Waiting works only when conditions favor you.

AWH language:

> **Situations ask, "What should we do?"**
> **Conditions answer, "Do we need to do anything at all?"**

The Cost of Situational Thinking

When decisions are made at the situational level:

- Cost is misjudged
- Risk is underestimated
- Timing is distorted

- Visibility increases unnecessarily
- Escalation becomes likely

Each of these is a failure mode already explored in this framework.

They share a common root: **failure to read conditions**.

Conditions Are Often Boring—and That Is the Signal

Conditions rarely announce themselves dramatically.

They appear as:

- Slight delays
- Minor friction
- Repeated misunderstandings
- Subtle resource drain
- Quiet morale decay

Situational thinkers ignore these until a crisis forces attention.

Sun Tzu never waits for crisis.

AWH principle:

What is boring today is often decisive tomorrow.

Diagnosing Conditions: The AWH Lens

The AWH framework forces condition analysis by asking questions that situations cannot answer.

For example:

- What costs are compounding regardless of action?
- Where is optionality shrinking?
- Who is under time pressure—and who is not?
- What information asymmetries persist?
- Where does visibility create vulnerability?

Situations do not reveal these answers.
Frameworks do.

Why Situations Feel Actionable—and Conditions Do Not

Situations feel actionable because they are discrete.

You can respond to an email.
You can address a complaint.
You can counter a move.

Conditions require:

- Structural change
- Patience
- Restraint

- Often, non-action

This makes condition-based strategy psychologically harder.

Sun Tzu accepts this difficulty as the price of effectiveness.

> "He who knows when he can fight and when he
> cannot, will be victorious."

Knowing when you *cannot* fight is condition awareness.

Situations Are Often Manufactured

Many situations are not organic. They are created intentionally to force reaction.

Examples:

- Provocations
- Deadlines
- Public challenges
- Artificial crises

Sun Tzu warns about this explicitly:

> "The general who is choleric and quick-tempered may
> be provoked by insults."

Provocations are situational weapons designed to override condition analysis.

AWH language:

> **If a situation demands immediate action, assume
> it was designed to.**

Conditions Explain Why "Reasonable" Decisions Fail

One of the most confusing experiences in leadership and strategy is making a decision that seemed reasonable—and watching it fail anyway.

The explanation is almost always conditional.

The decision addressed the situation.
The conditions remained hostile.

Sun Tzu never evaluates decisions in isolation. He evaluates alignment.

AWH principle:

> **A correct decision in hostile conditions is still a
> bad decision.**

Reading Conditions Across Time

Situations are momentary.
Conditions persist.

This makes time a diagnostic tool.

Questions like:

- Has this pattern appeared before?
- Does friction recur in the same place?
- Are the same resources always strained?

Reveal conditions.

Sun Tzu's aversion to prolonged warfare reflects time-based condition awareness.

Conditions and Non-Decision

When conditions are favorable, action may be unnecessary.
When conditions are unfavorable, action may be fatal.

This leads to one of the most counterintuitive strategic disciplines: **choosing not to decide**.

Sun Tzu legitimizes this repeatedly.

> "If the enemy is in superior strength, evade him."

Evading is not responding to the situation. It is respecting the condition.

Why Frameworks Matter More Than Intelligence

Intelligence often improves situational awareness.

Frameworks improve condition diagnosis.

That is why this book does not teach tactics.

AWH language:

> **Intelligence tells you what is happening.**
> **Frameworks tell you what matters.**

Common Misread: "But This Situation Is Different"

Every failure claims uniqueness.

"This time is different."
"These conditions don't apply here."

Sun Tzu heard this argument long before it was modern.

He rejected it.

> "In the midst of chaos, there is also opportunity."

Chaos does not eliminate conditions. It reveals them.

AWH principle:

Situations differ. Conditions rhyme.

From Reaction to Diagnosis

This chapter exists to shift the reader's default mode.

From:

- Reaction → response → escalation

To:

- Diagnosis → alignment → resolution

Sun Tzu's work performs this shift implicitly. AWH makes it explicit.

The Discipline of Ignoring Situations

This does not mean ignoring reality.

It means refusing to be governed by surface-level stimuli.

Sun Tzu's generals do not ignore battles. They ignore **panic about battles**.

AWH language:

> **Ignoring situations is not denial.**
> **It is prioritization.**

Diagnostic Questions That Reveal Conditions

Before responding to any situation, the framework demands:

- What condition allowed this situation to arise?
- Does responding change that condition—or reinforce it?
- Who benefits more from immediate response?
- What happens if nothing is done?

Situational answers are emotional.
Conditional answers are strategic.

Closing Orientation

This chapter establishes one of the deepest distinctions in the entire framework:

**Situations are what you see.
Conditions are what decide.**

Sun Tzu never fought situations.
He shaped conditions until situations resolved themselves.

Ancient Wisdom Hacks makes the discipline explicit:

**If you find yourself constantly responding to situations, you are already behind.
If you are shaping conditions, situations become irrelevant.**

Strategy is not the art of handling crises.
It is the discipline of ensuring crises never gain leverage.

That is the difference between reacting to the visible—and mastering the invisible.

Chapter 20

Re-Reading Under Pressure

Introduction: Why the Same Text Says Something Different When Stakes Rise

Most people believe understanding is stable.

They assume that once something is learned, it remains accessible—unchanged by circumstance, emotion, or pressure. They believe clarity is a property of information itself.

This belief is false.

Understanding is **state-dependent**.

What you comprehend calmly is not what you comprehend under pressure. What seems obvious in preparation becomes ambiguous in crisis. What appeared disciplined becomes optional when urgency intrudes.

This is not a failure of intelligence. It is a failure to account for **how pressure reshapes perception**.

The Art of War anticipates this problem with unsettling precision. Sun Tzu does not write to inspire insight in calm moments. He writes to preserve clarity **when clarity is hardest to maintain**.

This chapter examines why meaning degrades under stress, why re-reading principles under pressure often leads to misinterpretation, and why **structure—not brilliance—is the only defense against cognitive collapse**.

The core premise is simple and uncomfortable:

> **If a framework cannot be read correctly under pressure, it is not a framework—it is a comfort object.**

Calm Reading vs. Pressured Reading

Calm Reading

In calm conditions:

- Time feels available
- Stakes feel abstract
- Identity feels secure
- Options appear plentiful

Under these conditions, principles are interpreted expansively. Nuance is accessible. Tradeoffs feel negotiable.

Calm reading produces *the illusion of mastery*.

People say:

- "Of course restraint matters."

- "Obviously timing is critical."
- "Yes, cost must be controlled first."

Agreement is easy when nothing is at risk.

Pressured Reading

Under pressure:

- Time compresses
- Stakes feel existential
- Identity feels threatened
- Options appear binary

The same words are now filtered through:

- Fear of loss
- Desire for control
- Urgency to act
- Need to appear decisive

Meaning narrows. Ambiguity becomes intolerable. Conditional language is ignored.

AWH language names the difference directly:

Calm reading is interpretive.
Pressured reading is selective.

Under stress, people do not read what is written. They read **what justifies movement**.

Why Pressure Changes Meaning

Pressure does not erase knowledge.
It **reorders priority**.

Under stress, the mind:

- Overweights immediate threats
- Undervalues long-term cost
- Simplifies complex tradeoffs
- Seeks relief, not accuracy

This is not a flaw. It is an evolutionary survival response.

Sun Tzu understood this centuries ago. That is why *The Art of War* is not written as situational advice, motivational rhetoric, or tactical instruction. It is written as **constraint language**—language that resists reinterpretation when pressure mounts.

> "Move not unless you see an advantage; use not your troops unless there is something to be gained."

This sentence is difficult to misread—even when stressed—*if* it is treated as a rule rather than a suggestion.

AWH principle:

> **Pressure does not create bad ideas.**
> **It reveals which ideas were never structurally fixed.**

The Illusion of "Knowing" a Principle

Many people claim to "know" Sun Tzu.

They quote him.
They reference him.
They agree with him.

And then they violate him the moment pressure appears.

Why?

Because knowledge that is not **proceduralized** collapses under stress.

Understanding must be:

- Ordered
- Gated
- Non-negotiable

Otherwise, it becomes optional.

Sun Tzu does not rely on the reader's judgment under pressure. He removes judgment wherever possible.

> "The general who wins a battle makes many calculations in his temple before the battle is fought."

This is not advice. It is **a sequencing requirement** designed to survive emotional interference.

AWH language is explicit:

**If a principle requires interpretation under stress,
it will be reinterpreted.**

How Pressure Rewrites Familiar Text

Under pressure, people unconsciously rewrite principles to fit their emotional state.

Examples:

- "Restraint matters" becomes "Restraint matters, *but this is different.*"
- "Timing is critical" becomes "Timing is critical, *so we must act now.*"
- "Visibility is dangerous" becomes "Visibility is dangerous, *but we need to signal strength.*"

Nothing was denied. Everything was reinterpreted.

Sun Tzu anticipated this exact failure mode.

> "The general who is choleric and quick-tempered may be provoked by insults."

Provocation works by forcing **reinterpretation under pressure**.

AWH principle:

**Stress does not silence principles.
It makes them negotiable.**

Unless structure forbids it.

Why Re-Reading Under Pressure Is Dangerous

Many people attempt to solve pressure-induced confusion by revisiting source material.

They re-read.
They quote again.
They look for reassurance.

This often makes the problem worse.

Why?

Because under pressure, re-reading becomes **confirmation seeking**, not comprehension.

The reader looks for:

- Justification for action
- Validation of urgency
- Language that permits movement

And finds it—even where it does not exist.

Sun Tzu's text is famously compact. Its density invites selective emphasis.

Without a framework, re-reading becomes **weaponized interpretation**.

AWH language is blunt:

> **Re-reading without structure increases confidence, not accuracy.**

Calm Insight vs. Operational Clarity

Insight feels powerful.
Clarity is operational.

Calm reading produces insight.
Pressure demands clarity.

The difference matters.

Insight:

- Explains
- Illuminates
- Inspires

Clarity:

- Constrains
- Orders
- Prevents error

Sun Tzu is uninterested in insight for its own sake. He wants **error prevention under pressure**.

"In war, discipline is more important than numbers."

Discipline here means **adherence to order when instinct says otherwise**.

AWH principle:

> **Insight is fragile.**
> **Structure is durable.**

Why Structure Is the Only Defense

Pressure collapses discretionary judgment.

What remains are:

- Habits
- Rules
- Defaults

This is true in combat, negotiation, leadership, and crisis decision-making.

Sun Tzu does not attempt to make generals wiser under pressure. He attempts to make them **less free to err**.

That is why his system:

- Repeats the same constraints
- Emphasizes preparation over reaction
- Treats action as last resort

AWH language makes the implication explicit:

> **Under pressure, you will not rise to your principles.**
> **You will fall to your structure.**

If your structure allows reinterpretation, pressure will exploit it.

How Clarity Degrades Without Structure

Clarity does not disappear all at once.

It degrades in stages.

Stage 1: Compression

Nuance disappears. Tradeoffs feel binary.

"This is risky, *but* we must act."

Stage 2: Justification

Principles are reframed to support movement.

"Sun Tzu valued speed."

(He did—*after preparation*.)

Stage 3: Reordering

Sequence is inverted.

Action precedes cost. Visibility precedes preparation.

Stage 4: Identity Binding

The decision becomes personal.

Reversal becomes humiliation.

Sun Tzu designed his system to block each stage.

AWH principle:

> **Clarity does not vanish.**
> **It is crowded out by urgency.**

The False Comfort of Familiarity

Familiar texts feel safe under stress.

People return to what they recognize.

This is dangerous.

Familiarity creates **overconfidence**. Overconfidence accelerates reinterpretation.

Sun Tzu's writing avoids warmth, narrative, and inspiration precisely to prevent this effect. It does not comfort. It constrains.

AWH language:

Comforting frameworks fail when discomfort arrives.

Why Pressure Rewards Misreading

Misreading under pressure often produces short-term relief.

Action feels decisive.
Uncertainty narrows.
Responsibility feels discharged.

This creates a feedback loop:

- Pressure → action → relief → reinforcement

The long-term cost is hidden.

Sun Tzu refuses to optimize for relief.

> "There is no instance of a nation benefiting from prolonged warfare."

Prolonged warfare often begins with a single relieving decision.

AWH principle:

Pressure rewards decisions that feel good now and cost more later.

Structure exists to block that reward.

The Role of the Canonical Sequence Under Pressure

The canonical sequence is not an intellectual model.
It is a **pressure survival mechanism**.

Under stress:

- You do not debate sequence
- You do not reinterpret steps
- You do not skip gates

You follow order—or you fail.

This is why the sequence is non-negotiable.

AWH language:

> **Sequence replaces judgment when judgment is compromised.**

Sun Tzu does not trust the commander's emotional state. He trusts order.

Why "Context" Is a Pressure Excuse

Under pressure, people say:

- "Context matters."
- "This situation is unique."
- "The framework must adapt."

Context always matters.

Sequence does not.

Sun Tzu never adapts sequence to context. He adapts interpretation *within* sequence.

AWH principle:

Context changes inputs.
Pressure attacks order.

Do not confuse the two.

Reading for Permission vs. Reading for Constraint

Under calm conditions, people read for understanding.

Under pressure, they read for **permission**.

Permission to act.
Permission to escalate.
Permission to ignore restraint.

Sun Tzu's text resists this by denying permission entirely.

"Do not press a desperate foe too hard."

This is not situational advice. It is a boundary.

AWH language:

Good frameworks tell you what you are not allowed to do.

Especially when you most want to.

Why Tactical Texts Fail Under Pressure

Tactical advice collapses under pressure because it:

- Encourages improvisation
- Requires situational judgment
- Invites comparison and adaptation

Frameworks survive because they:

- Limit choice
- Enforce order
- Prevent early error

This is why *The Art of War* endures and most tactical manuals do not.

AWH principle:

> **Advice fails under stress.**
> **Structure survives.**

The Discipline of Pre-Commitment

Sun Tzu's system assumes pre-commitment.

You decide *in advance*:

- What you will not do
- What order you will follow
- What costs are unacceptable

This is why calculations happen "in the temple."

Once pressure arrives, the decision is no longer open.

AWH language:

> **Decide how you will decide before you need to decide.**

Otherwise, pressure decides for you.

Why This Framework Must Be Read Repeatedly

Repetition is not redundancy.

It is conditioning.

Under stress, what you recall is not what you learned once—it is what you rehearsed structurally.

Sun Tzu's aphoristic style supports this. The same ideas recur in different forms to reinforce order.

AWH principle:

> **Repetition builds defaults.**
> **Defaults determine behavior under pressure.**

The Illusion of "Staying Rational"

Many leaders believe they can "stay rational" under pressure.

This belief is itself a liability.

Sun Tzu does not assume rationality. He assumes vulnerability.

That is why his system:

- Reduces reliance on judgment
- Narrows acceptable actions

- Prefers inaction to impulsive motion

AWH language:

Rationality is not a state.
It is a structure.

Pressure as a Diagnostic Tool

Pressure reveals whether a framework is real.

If under stress:

- Sequence is violated
- Restraint is ignored
- Visibility is embraced
- Action is rushed

Then the framework was decorative.

Sun Tzu's work survives because it was written for commanders who would read it **when their lives depended on not misreading it**.

How to Read This Framework Correctly Under Pressure

Not by searching for insight.
Not by looking for justification.
Not by rereading selectively.

But by asking only:

- What step of the sequence am I in?
- What step am I trying to skip?
- What cost am I trying not to see?

If those questions are answered honestly, clarity returns.

Closing Orientation

This chapter exists as a warning.

Not about misunderstanding *The Art of War*—but about misunderstanding **yourself under pressure**.

Sun Tzu did not write for calm readers.
He wrote for leaders whose judgment would be tested when everything felt urgent.

Ancient Wisdom Hacks makes the implication explicit:

> **If your understanding of strategy changes under pressure, you never understood it structurally.**

Clarity does not survive stress by insight.
It survives by order.

And order must be decided **before** pressure makes
reinterpretation irresistible.

PART VI

RELATION TO OTHER FRAMEWORKS

(Why this framework is necessary but insufficient alone)

Chapter 21

What *The Art of War* Does Not Address

Introduction: The Limits of a Perfectly Cold System

One of the most dangerous ways to read **The Art of War** is to treat it as complete.

It is not.

It is precise.
It is durable.
It is structurally ruthless in its clarity.

But it is not total.

Sun Tzu gives us a decision system optimized for **survival, advantage, and cost control under adversarial pressure**. What he does *not* give us is equally important—because the failures that occur outside his frame often destroy those who apply his system flawlessly.

This chapter exists to define those boundaries.

Not to weaken *The Art of War*.
But to **prevent its misuse**.

The AWH framework treats Sun Tzu as a *necessary* foundation for strategy—but **insufficient alone** when decisions intersect with legitimacy, long-term power maintenance, human ego, coalition dynamics, and moral injury.

These are not oversights.
They are exclusions.

And ignoring them is how technically sound strategy collapses socially, politically, or psychologically *after* it has already succeeded.

Why Every Framework Has a Boundary

No framework governs reality in full.

Each governs a slice of it—optimizing for certain outcomes while deliberately ignoring others.

The Art of War optimizes for:

- Survival

- Advantage
- Cost minimization
- Conflict resolution

It deliberately **does not optimize for**:

- Moral coherence
- Political legitimacy
- Emotional integration
- Social meaning

Sun Tzu is not wrong for this. He is focused.

AWH language is explicit:

> **A framework that tries to do everything does nothing well.**

But a framework that is mistaken for total truth becomes dangerous.

What Sun Tzu Explicitly Optimizes For

Before naming what is missing, it is critical to restate what Sun Tzu *does* cover—and why he excludes other concerns.

Sun Tzu assumes:

- Adversarial conditions
- Scarce resources
- Asymmetric information

- High cost of error

Under those conditions, clarity must be cold.

> "War is a matter of vital importance to the State; the province of life or death; the road to survival or ruin."

This is the scope.

Within it, *The Art of War* is unmatched.

Outside it, it is silent.

---

1. Legitimacy

What Sun Tzu Does *Not* Address

Sun Tzu does not meaningfully address **legitimacy**—the social, moral, or political right to exercise power.

He assumes legitimacy exists or is irrelevant.

This is not negligence. It is an intentional abstraction.

Sun Tzu asks:

- Can you win?
- At what cost?
- With what exposure?

He does *not* ask:

- Should you be obeyed?
- Do others believe in your authority?
- Is your power accepted as rightful?

Why This Matters

A decision can be strategically optimal and
legitimacy-destroying.

Examples:

- Efficient restructuring that annihilates trust
- Perfectly timed consolidation that provokes revolt
- Silent domination that creates moral backlash

Sun Tzu would call these successes—until the backlash creates
new adversaries.

AWH language clarifies the risk:

> **Strategy can preserve position while destroying
> permission.**

Legitimacy frameworks—political theory, moral philosophy,
institutional trust—must sit *beside* Sun Tzu, not beneath him.

---

2. Power Maintenance (Beyond Winning)

Sun Tzu Ends Where Governance Begins

The Art of War is fundamentally about **winning without unnecessary cost**.

It is not about **maintaining power once conflict subsides**.

Sun Tzu assumes:

- After victory, order follows
- Authority consolidates naturally
- Resistance dissolves

History proves otherwise.

Power maintenance requires:

- Ritual
- Narrative
- Redistribution
- Inclusion
- Symbolic repair

None of these appear in Sun Tzu.

> "The supreme art of war is to subdue the enemy without fighting."

But what happens **after** subdual?

Sun Tzu does not say.

AWH principle:

> **Winning removes resistance.**
> **Governing must replace it.**

Without a governance framework, Sun Tzu's success creates a vacuum.

---

3. Human Ego

The Most Dangerous Exclusion

Sun Tzu understands ego as a *risk factor*.

He warns against:

- Choleric generals
- Prideful commanders
- Emotion-driven action

  "The general who is choleric and quick-tempered may be provoked by insults."

But he treats ego as something to be *controlled*, not *processed*.

What he does not address:

- Identity collapse after restraint
- Psychological recoil after suppression
- Ego rebound after victory

This matters because ego does not disappear when ignored. It **accumulates pressure**.

AWH language is blunt:

**Unacknowledged ego does not vanish.
It reemerges as sabotage, overreach, or collapse.**

Frameworks from psychology, leadership development, and ethics
are required to manage what Sun Tzu suppresses.

---

4. Coalition Pride

Sun Tzu Assumes Unity

Sun Tzu assumes command authority.

He assumes:

- Clear hierarchy
- Enforced discipline
- Aligned incentives

Coalitions violate all three.

Coalitions include:

- Multiple power centers
- Competing identities
- Pride not subordinated to efficiency

Sun Tzu does not address:

- Face-saving
- Symbolic equality
- Distributed legitimacy

In coalitions, *being right* is often less important than **allowing others to feel intact**.

AWH language:

> **Coalitions do not break from bad strategy.**
> **They break from wounded pride.**

Sun Tzu's silence here is not a flaw—it is a boundary.

---

5. Moral Injury

The Cost Sun Tzu Does Not Count

Sun Tzu counts:

- Material cost
- Strategic cost
- Opportunity cost

He does not count **moral injury**—the internal damage caused by actions that violate personal or collective values.

Examples:

- Leaders who win but cannot live with the methods
- Organizations that succeed while hollowing meaning
- Individuals who retain power but lose coherence

Sun Tzu is unconcerned with this dimension.

He optimizes outcomes, not inner alignment.

AWH principle:

> **Moral injury does not prevent victory.**
> **It prevents continuation.**

Frameworks from ethics, psychology, spirituality, and restorative justice are required here.

Why These Gaps Are Dangerous If Ignored

When *The Art of War* is treated as total:

- Legitimacy collapses silently
- Power becomes brittle
- Ego rebounds destructively
- Coalitions fracture
- Leaders burn out or radicalize

None of these failures contradict Sun Tzu.

They occur **outside his scope**.

AWH language is precise:

> **Sun Tzu prevents strategic error.**
> **He does not prevent human fallout.**

The Error of Moralizing Sun Tzu

Some readers attempt to retrofit morality into *The Art of War*.

This is a mistake.

Sun Tzu is not immoral.
He is **amoral by design**.

He assumes survival precedes morality.

> "War is a matter of life and death."

This framing is honest—but incomplete for modern leadership.

AWH principle:

> **Do not ask Sun Tzu to be ethical.**
> **Ask ethics to constrain Sun Tzu.**

Why This Framework Still Depends on Sun Tzu

Despite these gaps, *The Art of War* remains irreplaceable.

Why?

Because:

- No ethical framework survives catastrophic miscalculation
- No legitimacy matters if the system collapses
- No moral system compensates for strategic incompetence

Sun Tzu gives you **survivability**.

Everything else presupposes survival.

How AWH Positions Sun Tzu Correctly

Ancient Wisdom Hacks does not elevate Sun Tzu above all frameworks.

It **anchors** him.

Sun Tzu governs:

- Decision order
- Cost discipline
- Risk containment
- Timing
- Restraint

Other frameworks must govern:

- Meaning
- Legitimacy
- Healing
- Power continuity

AWH language:

Sun Tzu is the skeleton.
Other frameworks are organs.

Mistake either for the whole body, and the system fails.

When to Step Outside Sun Tzu Consciously

Leaders must know when *not* to apply Sun Tzu directly.

Examples:

- Healing a wounded organization
- Rebuilding trust after conflict
- Addressing moral fallout
- Maintaining coalition cohesion

Using *The Art of War* in these moments often causes harm—not because it is wrong, but because it is misapplied.

The Danger of "Winning Too Cleanly"

One of the strangest modern failures is this:

A leader wins strategically…
And destroys their ability to lead afterward.

Why?

Because Sun Tzu does not concern himself with **how victory is received**.

AWH language:

> **A victory that leaves no space for dignity creates permanent resistance.**

Sun Tzu avoids this by recommending non-fighting victories—but he does not explain how dignity is restored.

That work belongs elsewhere.

Integrating Without Diluting

The solution is not to soften Sun Tzu.

It is to **contain him**.

Use his framework to:

- Decide *whether* and *when* to act
- Prevent irreversible error
- Avoid catastrophic loss

Then use other frameworks to:

- Legitimize outcomes
- Sustain authority

- Repair meaning

AWH principle:

> **Cold strategy first.**
> **Human repair second.**

Reverse the order, and you risk collapse.

Closing Orientation

This chapter exists to prevent a common and catastrophic misunderstanding:

> *That mastering The Art of War is enough.*

It is not.

Sun Tzu tells you how to survive conflict with minimal loss.
He does not tell you how to live with what survival costs.

Ancient Wisdom Hacks makes the boundary explicit:

> **Use Sun Tzu to avoid disaster.**
> **Use other frameworks to remain human.**

Only by respecting what *The Art of War* does **not** address can you use it responsibly—without turning strategic clarity into long-term damage.

That is not a weakness of the framework.

It is proof of its honesty.

Chapter 22

Why *The Prince* Is Required

Introduction: When Strategy Succeeds but Power Fails

There is a dangerous illusion at the center of many strategic victories.

The illusion is this:
that once the correct decision is made, the problem is solved.

It is not.

Correct decisions can win conflicts.
They can resolve engagements.
They can minimize cost and avoid disaster.

And still leave power **unstable**, authority **contested**, and legitimacy **fragile**.

This is where **The Prince** becomes unavoidable.

Where **The Art of War** governs *decision under adversarial pressure*, *The Prince* governs **power after the decision has already been made**.

This chapter exists to formalize a hard truth:

Strategy can win the moment.
Power must survive what follows.

Sun Tzu helps you avoid catastrophe.
Machiavelli helps you avoid irrelevance.

Both are required.

The Core Distinction: Decision vs. Power

The Art of War is a **decision framework**.
The Prince is a **power framework**.

They solve different problems.

Sun Tzu asks:

- Should you act?
- At what cost?
- With what risk?
- Under what conditions?

Machiavelli asks:

- Will authority persist?
- Will obedience remain?
- Will legitimacy survive resentment?
- Will power endure memory?

AWH language makes the boundary explicit:

> **Sun Tzu governs action.**
> **Machiavelli governs consequence.**

Confusing the two leads to failure after success.

Power Persists Beyond Decisions

Decisions are discrete.
Power is continuous.

A decision ends when action is taken.
Power continues indefinitely—absorbing the effects of that action.

Sun Tzu's system is optimized to **end things**:

- End conflict
- End exposure
- End escalation
- End unnecessary cost

Machiavelli's system is optimized to **continue things**:

- Continue obedience
- Continue authority
- Continue legitimacy
- Continue stability

This difference matters.

AWH principle:

The longer the time horizon, the less sufficient decision logic becomes.

Power is what remains when the decision is no longer visible.

Why Sun Tzu Is Silent on Power Maintenance

Sun Tzu assumes a unified state with:

- Accepted hierarchy
- Clear command authority
- Enforceable discipline

Within that assumption, power maintenance is trivial.

> "If soldiers are punished before they have grown attached to you, they will not prove submissive."

This is the extent of his concern.

He does not address:

- Factional loyalty
- Public legitimacy
- Narrative control
- Institutional decay

Because those are not problems of *war*.
They are problems of **rule**.

Machiavelli writes precisely where Sun Tzu stops.

Authority Survives Outcomes

One of the most counterintuitive truths in leadership is this:

You can win—and lose authority.

You can succeed—and weaken power.

You can be correct—and be overthrown.

Sun Tzu does not consider this paradox. Machiavelli is obsessed with it.

> "Men judge more by the eye than by the hand,
> because everyone can see, but few can feel."

Authority is perception stabilized over time.

AWH language clarifies the danger:

> **Correct outcomes do not guarantee continued obedience.**

Power survives outcomes only if it is actively maintained.

The Failure Mode: Strategically Correct, Politically Dead

History is full of leaders who applied Sun Tzu flawlessly and still failed.

They:

- Eliminated rivals efficiently
- Avoided unnecessary conflict
- Minimized cost
- Controlled exposure

And then lost power.

Why?

Because Sun Tzu does not teach:

- How to manage resentment
- How to preserve dignity of the defeated
- How to integrate elites
- How to signal legitimacy

Machiavelli does.

> "Injuries ought to be done all at once, so that, being tasted less, they offend less."

This is not cruelty.
It is **power preservation logic**.

Legitimacy Constrains Future Choices

Sun Tzu treats future choices as functions of:

- Resources
- Risk
- Timing
- Position

Machiavelli adds another constraint:

Legitimacy.

Legitimacy determines:

- What actions are tolerated
- Which costs provoke revolt
- When force becomes self-defeating
- How much coercion is sustainable

AWH language:

> **Legitimacy is not morality.**
> **It is permission.**

Without permission, every future decision costs more.

Why Power Cannot Be Treated as a One-Time Win

Strategy culture often assumes:

- Win once, rule forever
- Decide correctly, and authority follows
- Remove opposition, and stability emerges

Machiavelli rejects this entirely.

> "A prince who is not wise himself cannot be well advised."

Wisdom here is not decision accuracy.
It is **continuous power calibration**.

AWH principle:

Power decays unless actively managed.

Sun Tzu prevents collapse.
Machiavelli prevents erosion.

The Emotional Dimension Sun Tzu Ignores

Sun Tzu treats emotion as noise.

"The general who is choleric and quick-tempered may be provoked by insults."

He warns against emotion—but does not manage it.

Machiavelli assumes emotion is unavoidable.

Fear, loyalty, resentment, pride—these are **materials of power**, not distractions.

"It is much safer to be feared than loved, if one must choose."

This is not advice to terrorize.
It is an acknowledgment of emotional reality.

AWH language bridges the gap:

**Sun Tzu suppresses emotion.
Machiavelli accounts for it.**

Both are required.

Coalition Pride and Elite Management

Sun Tzu assumes obedience.
Machiavelli assumes **elites**.

Elites:

- Remember slights

- Measure status
- Protect dignity
- Coordinate resistance

Sun Tzu does not teach how to manage elite pride.

Machiavelli does—explicitly.

> "He who becomes prince by the favor of the nobles
> must keep them friendly."

This matters because:

- Coalitions fracture silently
- Power collapses suddenly
- Strategic brilliance cannot repair wounded pride

AWH principle:

> **Power fails more often from elite resentment than
> from enemy strength.**

Why Legitimacy Is a Strategic Asset

Legitimacy:

- Lowers enforcement cost
- Reduces resistance
- Preserves optionality
- Extends time horizons

Sun Tzu lowers cost through **avoidance**.
Machiavelli lowers cost through **acceptance**.

Different mechanisms. Same objective.

AWH language:

> **Force buys compliance.**
> **Legitimacy buys time.**

Without time, no strategy survives.

When Sun Tzu Alone Becomes Dangerous

Sun Tzu applied without Machiavelli produces leaders who are:

- Cold
- Efficient
- Unforgiving
- Structurally correct

And eventually isolated.

They win engagements and lose allegiance.

They optimize for cost and ignore memory.

Machiavelli exists to correct this imbalance.

The Prince as a Post-Decision Framework

The Prince does not tell you **whether** to act.

It tells you how to **live with what you have done**.

It governs:

- Reputation after action
- Narrative after conflict
- Integration after victory
- Constraint after dominance

AWH principle:

> **Sun Tzu decides the move.**
> **Machiavelli decides the aftermath.**

The Misreading of Machiavelli

Machiavelli is often caricatured as cynical or immoral.

This is incorrect.

He is **contextually honest**.

He assumes:

- People remember harm

- Power invites challenge
- Virtue is judged by outcome
- Stability matters more than intention

Sun Tzu assumes:

- Conflict must be ended efficiently

Neither is complete alone.

Why Authority Must Survive Even Good Decisions

A good decision that destroys authority creates long-term vulnerability.

Examples:

- Layoffs handled efficiently but cruelly
- Reforms enacted correctly but without consent
- Strategic withdrawals perceived as weakness

Sun Tzu minimizes loss.
Machiavelli minimizes backlash.

AWH language:

A decision that weakens authority raises the cost of every future decision.

Integrating Sun Tzu and Machiavelli Correctly

The integration is sequential—not blended.

1. Use Sun Tzu to decide:
   - Whether to act
   - When to act
   - At what cost
   - With what exposure
2. Use Machiavelli to manage:
   - Perception
   - Legitimacy
   - Elite alignment
   - Narrative continuity

Never reverse the order.

AWH principle:

Cold strategy first.
Power maintenance second.

The Failure of Pure Ethics Without Power

Ethical frameworks without power realism collapse.

Sun Tzu prevents disaster.
Machiavelli prevents naivety.

AWH language:

> **Ethics without power dies.**
> **Power without ethics rots.**

This chapter does not moralize Machiavelli.
It contextualizes him.

Why This Framework Still Rejects Tactics

Neither Sun Tzu nor Machiavelli give tactics in the modern sense.

They give **constraints**.

That is why both endure.

AWH language:

> **Tactics expire.**
> **Power dynamics persist.**

The Cost of Ignoring Machiavelli

Leaders who ignore Machiavelli:

- Win once
- Lose slowly
- Become brittle
- Are replaced quietly

Not by enemies—but by insiders.

Sun Tzu cannot prevent this.

Closing Orientation

This chapter establishes why **The Prince is required**—not as a replacement for Sun Tzu, but as a necessary continuation.

Sun Tzu teaches you how to survive decisions.
Machiavelli teaches you how to survive success.

Ancient Wisdom Hacks makes the final distinction explicit:

> **If you only know how to decide, you will be outlasted by those who know how to rule.**

Power does not end when the battle does.
Authority does not emerge automatically from correctness.
Legitimacy is not a side effect of victory.

Strategy gets you through the moment.
Power determines whether you remain standing afterward.

That is why *The Prince* is not optional.

Chapter 23

Why *The Iliad* Is Required

Introduction: Where Perfect Strategy Still Fails

There is a final illusion that must be destroyed.

The illusion is this:
that if a decision system is sufficiently rigorous, human failure can be engineered away.

It cannot.

Even when decisions are correct.
Even when sequence is followed.
Even when cost is minimized and risk is bounded.

Humans still break systems.

This is where **The Iliad** becomes indispensable.

Where **The Art of War** governs *decision under pressure*, and **The Prince** governs *power after action*, *The Iliad* governs **the human fracture that neither system can prevent**.

This chapter formalizes the final, uncomfortable truth:

Strategy fails not only because of bad decisions or unstable power—but because humans break alignment even when everything else is correct.

Sun Tzu prevents catastrophe.
Machiavelli preserves authority.
Homer explains why, even then, collapse still happens.

The Domain Homer Owns

The Iliad is not a strategy manual.
It is not a leadership guide.
It is not a decision framework.

It is something far more dangerous and more necessary:

A record of **what humans do inside systems they did not design—and often cannot emotionally survive**.

Homer does not explain how wars are won.
He explains why wars continue long after winning no longer matters.

AWH language defines Homer's domain precisely:

Homer governs the cost that cannot be modeled.

Humans Break Systems

Every system assumes compliance.

Even Sun Tzu's coldest logic assumes:

- Discipline holds
- Orders are followed
- Command is respected
- Restraint is obeyed

The Iliad shows us what happens when this assumption fails.

The Trojan War does not spiral because of bad tactics.
It spirals because of **wounded pride, dishonor, grief, rage, and identity collapse**.

Achilles does not withdraw because the strategy is wrong.
He withdraws because **his honor is violated**.

> "You shameless schemer, with your mind forever on profit… how can any Achaean obey you gladly?"

This is not a tactical complaint.
It is a human rupture.

AWH principle:

> **Systems fail at the point where humans stop consenting internally—even if they still obey externally.**

Pride Destroys Alignment

Alignment is not agreement.
It is **felt legitimacy**.

Sun Tzu engineers alignment through discipline.
Machiavelli maintains alignment through power and perception.

Homer shows alignment collapsing from the inside.

Achilles and Agamemnon are nominally on the same side.
They share objectives.
They face a common enemy.

And still the system breaks.

Why?

Because pride is wounded.

> "He has taken my prize and dishonored me."

This single injury costs the Achaeans more lives than any Trojan tactic.

AWH language is uncompromising:

> **Pride can destroy alignment faster than incompetence ever could.**

Why Strategy Cannot Suppress Pride

Sun Tzu warns against pride.
Machiavelli manages it.

Neither resolves it.

Pride is not an error.
It is a **structural feature of human identity**.

In *The Iliad*:

- Achilles' pride overrides collective survival
- Agamemnon's pride overrides reconciliation
- Hector's pride overrides retreat
- Patroclus' pride overrides restraint

Every major disaster in the epic traces back to pride mismanaged.

AWH principle:

> **Where pride is ignored, strategy becomes brittle.**

Cost Is Paid by People, Not Models

Strategy counts cost.

Models quantify:

- Resources
- Time

- Risk
- Opportunity

The Iliad reveals what those models leave out.

Cost is paid in:

- Grief
- Trauma
- Moral injury
- Broken bonds
- Survivor guilt

When Achilles returns to battle, he does not do so strategically.

He does so in rage.

> "So he spoke, and grief yet more possessed his
> spirit."

This grief produces slaughter—but no resolution.

Sun Tzu would call Achilles' return irrational.
Machiavelli would call it destabilizing.

Homer calls it **inevitable**.

AWH language clarifies the blind spot:

> **Models track outcomes.**
> **Humans carry consequences.**

Why Winning Does Not Heal Humans

One of the most dangerous myths in leadership and conflict is that victory heals trauma.

The Iliad rejects this completely.

Troy falls—but nothing is healed.

Achilles wins—but loses Patroclus, Hector, and himself.

> "Thus spoke he, and rent with his hands his hair."

Victory compounds loss.

AWH principle:

> **Success resolves problems.**
> **It does not resolve pain.**

This distinction matters because unresolved pain returns as:

- Sabotage
- Overreach
- Collapse
- Moral decay

Moral Injury: The Cost After the Cost

Sun Tzu minimizes loss.
Machiavelli manages fallout.

Homer shows **what remains anyway**.

Moral injury occurs when actions:

- Violate personal values
- Destroy meaning
- Fracture identity

Achilles is not undone by defeat.
He is undone by **what he becomes while winning**.

AWH language:

> **Moral injury is the debt strategy does not
> record—but always collects.**

Why Discipline Alone Fails

Sun Tzu emphasizes discipline.

"In war, discipline is more important than numbers."

Discipline works—until identity breaks.

Achilles is disciplined.
He is peerless in combat.
He follows the rules of honor as he understands them.

And still he refuses to fight.

Why?

Because discipline cannot repair **humiliation**.

AWH principle:

> **Discipline governs behavior.**
> **Pride governs allegiance.**

The Limits of Power Over Humans

Machiavelli understands fear and love.
He manages elites and obedience.

Homer shows the moment where:

- Fear fails
- Love collapses
- Authority becomes irrelevant

Agamemnon is king.
He commands armies.

He cannot command Achilles' soul.

AWH language:

> **Power controls bodies.**
> **It does not command meaning.**

When meaning collapses, systems fracture silently before they
break visibly.

Coalition Failure Through Human Fracture

The Trojan War is a coalition war.

It fails repeatedly because:

- Pride outranks purpose
- Status outranks survival
- Insult outranks strategy

Homer's lesson is brutal:

> **Coalitions die emotionally before they die strategically.**

Sun Tzu assumes coalition discipline.
Machiavelli manages coalition incentives.

Homer shows what happens when neither touches **honor**.

Why Grief Is Strategically Relevant

Grief is invisible to models.

And yet it shapes outcomes decisively.

Achilles' grief produces:

- Reckless violence
- Desecration of Hector's body
- Further alienation
- Spiritual collapse

> "So he spoke, and pity for the grey-haired sire seized him."

Only when Achilles confronts shared grief does restraint return.

This is not a tactical moment.
It is a human one.

AWH principle:

> **Grief ignored becomes rage.**
> **Rage destabilizes systems.**

Why *The Iliad* Cannot Be Replaced

No amount of psychology replaces Homer.

Because *The Iliad* does not explain humans—it **shows them breaking**.

It refuses:

- Redemption arcs
- Clean victories
- Moral resolution

It forces confrontation with cost beyond calculation.

AWH language:

Homer is required because he refuses closure.

Strategy wants closure.
Humans rarely get it.

When Leaders Fail Without Homer

Leaders who master Sun Tzu and Machiavelli but ignore Homer
often become:

- Cold
- Isolated
- Effective
- Hollow

They win decisions.
They hold power.

And then implode—or rot from within.

Why?

Because they treat people as:

- Variables
- Incentives
- Risks

Homer reminds us:

> **People are not inputs.**
> **They are the terrain strategy crosses.**

Why Pride Must Be Seen, Not Suppressed

Sun Tzu suppresses pride.
Machiavelli redirects it.

Homer confronts it.

Achilles' pride is not negotiated away.
It is honored, wounded, and finally reconciled—too late.

AWH principle:

> **Unacknowledged pride does not disappear.**
> **It metastasizes.**

Cost Is Paid in Blood, Memory, and Silence

The Trojan War lasts ten years.

Not because it must—but because no one can let go.

Homer records:

- Endless funerals
- Repeated grief
- Cycles of revenge

Sun Tzu would end the war.
Machiavelli would consolidate power.

Homer shows why neither fully succeeds.

AWH language:

Systems seek efficiency.
Humans seek meaning.

When meaning is destroyed, efficiency accelerates collapse.

Why This Framework Needs Homer Last

Homer is placed last deliberately.

Because:

- He cannot guide decisions
- He cannot preserve power
- He cannot prevent conflict

What he can do is **prevent self-deception**.

He reminds the strategist:

- Who pays the cost
- What remains after victory
- Why restraint matters even when unnecessary
- Why cruelty echoes longer than success

AWH principle:

Homer does not tell you how to win.
He tells you what winning costs humans.

Integrating All Three Correctly

The correct order is not philosophical.
It is structural.

1. **Sun Tzu** — Prevent catastrophe
2. **Machiavelli** — Preserve power
3. **Homer** — Remember humanity

Never reverse it.

But never omit the last.

AWH language:

Cold strategy without power collapses.
Power without humanity corrodes.

The Final Warning

If you master strategy and power without Homer:

- You will succeed
- You will endure
- You will be obeyed

And you may destroy:

- Loyalty
- Meaning
- Yourself

Homer is not optional.

He is the cost ledger strategy refuses to keep.

Closing Orientation

This chapter completes the framework's outer boundary.

Sun Tzu teaches you how to decide without dying.
Machiavelli teaches you how to rule without being overthrown.
Homer teaches you why even then, humans bleed, break, and remember.

Ancient Wisdom Hacks makes the final truth explicit:

If you want to build systems that survive reality, you must account for the fact that humans are not systems.

They carry pride.
They carry grief.
They carry memory.

And no framework—no matter how brilliant—escapes that debt.

Ignoring Homer does not make strategy cleaner.

It only makes the bill come due later,
paid not in models—

but in people.

CLOSING

The Role of the *Art of War* Framework

Final Positioning: What This Framework Actually Is

By the time a reader reaches this point, one misunderstanding must be removed completely:

The Art of War is not a worldview.

It is not a belief system.
It is not a leadership identity.
It is not a philosophy of life.

It is a **machine**.

Cold.
Impersonal.
Unsentimental.

And deliberately incomplete.

The Art of War survives not because it inspires greatness, but because it **prevents irreversible error**. It does not elevate the user. It constrains them. It does not reward courage. It punishes waste.

This closing chapter exists to lock the framework into its proper role—so it is used correctly, limited intentionally, and never mistaken for something it was never meant to be.

The Art of War Framework is not about becoming powerful.

It is about **not destroying yourself while attempting to act**.

The Core Function: A Decision Engine

At its heart, the Art of War Framework is a **decision engine**.

It processes:

- Constraint
- Cost
- Risk
- Timing
- Preparation
- Visibility
- Restraint

And produces one of two outputs:

- **Do nothing**
- **Act—only if total cost decreases**

That is all.

It does not generate vision.
It does not create ambition.
It does not supply purpose.

Sun Tzu never asks what you *want*.
He asks whether what you are about to do is survivable.

> "Move not unless you see an advantage; use not your
> troops unless there is something to be gained."

This is not motivation.
It is a logic gate.

AWH language states it plainly:

> **The framework does not help you choose goals.
> It helps you avoid dying while pursuing them.**

A Cost Containment System, Not a Victory Machine

Modern readers obsess over winning.

Sun Tzu obsesses over **cost**.

He returns to it repeatedly:

- Prolonged war exhausts states
- Sieges consume strength
- Escalation compounds loss

- Visibility attracts resistance

"There is no instance of a nation benefiting from prolonged warfare."

This is not a moral claim.
It is an accounting statement.

The Art of War Framework is best understood as a **cost containment system** operating under adversarial pressure.

It exists to:

- Identify hidden cost
- Prevent compounding loss
- Preserve optionality
- Avoid terminal error

Victory is secondary.

AWH principle:

If victory increases total cost over time, it is strategically irrelevant.

Sun Tzu would rather avoid winning than win expensively.

A Pre-Action Discipline

The Art of War Framework operates **before action**.

Not during.
Not after.

Before.

It is explicitly hostile to improvisation under pressure.

> "The general who wins a battle makes many calculations in his temple before the battle is fought."

This line is the entire framework compressed.

Calculations happen:

- In calm
- In privacy
- Without urgency
- Without audience

Once pressure arrives, the framework is no longer active. Its job is already done.

AWH language makes the boundary explicit:

If you are still deciding while under pressure, the framework has already failed.

It exists to remove discretion *before* discretion becomes dangerous.

What the Framework Is Not (And Never Was)

Not a Leadership Philosophy

The Art of War does not teach:

- Inspiration
- Empathy
- Vision
- Cultural development
- Personal growth

Sun Tzu does not care if you are admired.
He cares if you survive contact.

Leadership philosophies address:

- Meaning
- Identity
- Motivation
- Belonging

The Art of War addresses **exposure to loss**.

AWH language:

> **If you use Sun Tzu to define your leadership identity, you will become brittle.**

Leadership requires warmth.
This framework is deliberately cold.

Not a Morality System

Sun Tzu does not define right and wrong.

He defines:

- Advantage
- Disadvantage
- Efficiency
- Waste

He is amoral by design.

> "War is a matter of life and death."

This framing excludes moral comfort.

As established earlier, morality must **constrain** Sun Tzu—not be derived from him.

AWH principle:

> **The Art of War keeps you alive.**
> **It does not tell you who you should be.**

Confusing the two leads to ethical collapse or moral rationalization.

Not a Playbook

Playbooks prescribe actions.

The Art of War prohibits most of them.

Sun Tzu does not tell you:

- How to attack
- Where to strike
- What tactics to use

He tells you when **not** to.

> "He will win who knows when to fight and when not to fight."

That is not instruction.
It is restraint encoded as doctrine.

AWH language:

> **If you are looking for moves, you are already misusing the framework.**

The framework exists to stop bad moves—not generate clever ones.

Why Boldness Is a Misread Outcome

Many modern readers equate strategy with boldness.

They expect:

- Decisive action
- Aggressive posture
- Assertive execution

Sun Tzu rejects this entirely.

Boldness increases:

- Visibility
- Resistance
- Escalation
- Cost

Sun Tzu prefers:

- Subtlety
- Delay
- Obscurity
- Restraint

> "Appear weak when you are strong, and strong when you are weak."

This is not bold.
It is **disciplined deception in service of cost reduction**.

AWH principle:

> **The framework does not make you brave.**
> **It makes you hard to damage.**

Precision as the True Output

Used correctly, the Art of War Framework produces **precision**.

Precision means:

- Acting less
- Acting later
- Acting smaller
- Acting only when asymmetry exists

Precision is boring.
Precision is quiet.
Precision rarely looks heroic.

And precision wins because it does not invite unnecessary response.

AWH language:

Precision is action reduced to necessity.

Sun Tzu's best victories are invisible.

> "To subdue the enemy without fighting is the acme of skill."

The absence of drama is the signal of correct use.

Why the Framework Must Remain Limited

One of the most important insights of this entire work is this:

The Art of War must remain incomplete to remain useful.

It must not expand into:

- Ethics
- Psychology
- Governance
- Meaning-making

Because once it tries to do those things, it loses its edge.

AWH principle:

> **A sharp tool becomes dangerous when mistaken for a whole system.**

Sun Tzu's value lies in what he refuses to address.

The Correct Stack (Reaffirmed)

The framework belongs in a stack—not at the top.

Correct ordering matters:

1. **The Art of War** — Prevent catastrophic decision error

2. **The Prince** — Maintain power and legitimacy after action
3. **The Iliad** — Account for human cost and fracture

Remove any layer, and the system fails differently.

But never invert them.

AWH language:

> **Cold discipline first.**
> **Power second.**
> **Humanity always last—but never omitted.**

The Most Common Misuse (Final Warning)

The most common misuse of the Art of War is this:

Using it to justify action.

Sun Tzu is not an accelerator.
He is a brake.

If you are quoting Sun Tzu to move faster, escalate harder, or dominate visibly, you have inverted his system.

AWH principle:

> **If Sun Tzu is being used to rationalize motion, he is being ignored.**

Correct use slows you down.

What Mastery Actually Looks Like

Mastery of this framework does not look impressive.

It looks like:

- Declined opportunities
- Unmade announcements
- Avoided conflicts
- Quiet exits
- Decisions never noticed

Sun Tzu's highest praise is silence.

AWH language:

> **When the framework is used correctly, nothing appears to happen.**

And that is the point.

Final Orientation

The Art of War Framework occupies a narrow, critical role:

It is:

- A decision engine
- A cost containment system
- A pre-action discipline

It is not:

- A leadership philosophy
- A morality system
- A playbook

It will not make you inspiring.
It will not make you righteous.
It will not make you admired.

Used correctly, it will make you **precise**.

And precision—not boldness—is what allows action to occur without triggering collapse.

Sun Tzu did not design a philosophy for living.

He designed a system for **not dying unnecessarily** when choices are constrained, information is incomplete, and cost compounds silently.

Ancient Wisdom Hacks leaves the reader with one final discipline:

> **Do not ask what this framework empowers you to do.**
> **Ask what it forbids you from doing.**

What remains after those prohibitions—that narrow, quiet margin of action—is where strategy actually lives.

Everything else is noise.

Final Page

Precision Is the Point

This book was not written to inspire you.
It was written to **prevent irreversible error**.

Most strategy books promise confidence, courage, or momentum.
This one promised none of those—by design.

What you have just completed is not a philosophy.
It is not a worldview.
It is not a playbook.

It is a **framework for deciding when *not* to act**—and for acting
only when action reduces total cost.

What This Book Actually Gave You

This work formalized **The Art of War** as it is meant to be used:

- A **decision engine**, not a source of wisdom
- A **cost containment system**, not a victory myth
- A **pre-action discipline**, not a motivational tool

You were not taught how to win.

You were taught how to:

- Detect hidden cost before it compounds
- Recognize when restraint is strength
- Avoid escalation traps that feel decisive but end careers
- Preserve optionality while others burn it
- Exit situations quietly instead of collapsing loudly

This framework does not reward boldness.
It punishes waste.

What This Book Refused to Do

Deliberately.

It did **not**:

- Tell you what goals to pursue
- Justify aggression or dominance
- Offer tactics disguised as insight
- Confuse confidence with clarity
- Pretend that strategy is the same as leadership, morality, or meaning

Those belong elsewhere.

This framework exists for one narrow purpose:

> **To help you survive decision pressure without destroying future choice.**

Who This Book Is For

This book is for people who already feel the cost of bad decisions:

- Founders who know that one move can poison the company
- Leaders who understand that visibility attracts resistance
- Operators who have watched "winning" quietly destroy leverage
- Strategists who no longer trust urgency
- Decision-makers who need fewer mistakes—not more bravado

If you are looking to feel powerful, this book will disappoint you.

If you are trying to **remain intact over time**, it will not.

How This Framework Is Meant to Be Used

Not once.
Not ceremonially.
Not quoted selectively.

It is meant to sit **between impulse and action**.

Before you announce.
Before you escalate.
Before you commit publicly.
Before you "just do something."

If it slows you down, it is working.
If it makes action rarer, it is working.
If it causes you to walk away quietly, it is working.

Correct use looks like nothing happened.

That is the signal.

The Final Truth

This framework will not make you admired.
It will not make you heroic.
It will not make you feel certain.

Used correctly, it will make you **precise**.

And precision—not boldness—is what allows people to act without triggering collapse, retaliation, or regret.

If this book leaves you calmer, more skeptical of urgency, and less interested in proving anything—then it has done its job.

Nothing else was promised.

Nothing else was needed.

THIS IS NOT A COLLECTION

This volume is part of **Ancient Wisdom Hacks**—
an ongoing body of work focused on how strategy, power, and failure actually function under pressure.

The books are only one layer.

What you are reading is an entry point into a larger system of interpretation, application, and expansion.

WHAT THESE WORKS ARE DESIGNED TO DO

Most people look for answers.

These works expose patterns:

- How decisions are made before they are visible
- How systems weaken before they collapse
- How power shifts before it is recognized

This is not theory.
It is applied observation.

THE SYSTEM BEHIND THE WORK

Across all volumes and future releases, three forces remain constant:

- **Strategy** — how outcomes are shaped before action
- **Conflict** — how people and systems break under pressure
- **Power** — how control is gained, maintained, and lost

No single book contains the full picture.
Each adds another angle.

CONTINUE BEYOND THIS VOLUME

New interpretations, applied volumes, and extended works are
released continuously.

To access current and future material, visit:

www.AncientWisdomHacks.com

WHAT YOU WILL FIND

- Additional applied volumes across industries
- Expanded interpretations of foundational texts
- New releases not available through standard distribution
- Future projects extending beyond books

The system is still expanding.

FINAL POSITION

Clarity does not make outcomes easier.

It removes the illusion that they were ever simple.

Ancient Wisdom Hacks
Interpretation over repetition.
Application over theory.